THE FIRST WORLD WAR A–Z

THE FIRST WORLD WAR

FROM ASSASSINATION TO ZEPPELIN — EVERYTHING YOU NEED TO KNOW

EDITOR | MARK HAWKINS-DADY
HISTORICAL CONSULTANT | TERRY CHARMAN

Published by IWM, Lambeth Road, London SE1 6HZ
iwm.org.uk

ISBN 978-1-904897-85-9

A catalogue record for this book is available from the
British Library
Printed and bound in Spain by Imago Publishing

All images © IWM unless otherwise stated
Cover design © www.ninataradesign.com
Internal design by James Alexander www.jadedesign.co.uk

Every effort has been made to contact all copyright
holders. The publishers will be glad to make good in future
editions any error or omissions brought to their attention.

10 9 8 7 6 5 4 3 2 1

MIX
Paper from
responsible sources
FSC® C051148

ACES *to*
AUSTRIA-HUNGARY

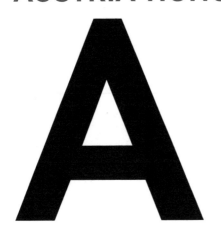

ACES

In the First World War, air fighting was a new and – to the press and public – exciting development. At first, **aeroplanes** were used for reconnaissance, but the desire to blind the enemy's 'eyes in the sky' and protect one's own planes produced a new breed: the fighter pilot. Their exploits were glamorised and celebrated, in particular those of the aces. The term was first coined by a French newspaper to describe Adolphe Pégoud and his high tally of enemy 'kills'. It was then used to mean any fighter pilot credited with shooting down a certain number of aircraft. In 1916 Britain found its first real ace in the shape of the young, seemingly fearless, Albert Ball. Although they were highly skilled and dedicated, aces were by no means immune to the dangers of combat, and the shocking attrition rates for pilots told their own story. Some of the most famous, such as Germany's **Red Baron**, Britain's Edward 'Mick' Mannock (and Ball himself), and France's Georges Guynemer, did not survive – brought down by enemy aircraft, ground fire or mechanical failure. Others though, including Germany's Hermann Goering and Ernst Udet, or New Zealander Arthur Coningham, lived on to shape the way aerial battles would be fought in the next war.

CW

AEROPLANES

The Wright brothers' historic first – a successful powered flight – had only been in 1903; yet by 1918 civilians had been bombed by aeroplanes, and over the **Western Front** hundreds of aircraft fought daily. A host of now legendary aircraft names had become common parlance, such as Britain's Sopwith Camel or Germany's Fokker Eindecker. On the eve of war, the European powers had begun to recognise the military potential of powered flight. Aerial reconnaissance – and soon aerial **photography** – became vital tools, providing a unique and (weather permitting) unobstructed view of the battlefield and even behind the lines. **Maps** could be made of battlefields and trench lines, troop movements could be monitored, and targets for artillery could be identified. It was no wonder that each side soon targeted the other's aircraft. When the Germans developed a method of synchronising the propeller with the **machine gun**, the age of the fighter **ace** was truly born. We tend to think of the air war as one of biplanes, but aeroplanes took all shapes and sizes, from monoplanes to the kind of triplane as flown by the **Red Baron** – though all airmen had to contend with the elements in their exposed cockpits. Many aircraft remained fragile constructions of a wooden skeleton with a fabric skin. But in 1918 the British four-engined, steel-reinforced 'Super Handley' was gearing up to drop a 3,000lb bombload on Berlin. Without the necessities of war, such rapid development would have been unthinkable.

MJP

AFRICA

By 1914, almost all of Africa was colonised by Europe's powers, which brought the continent immediately into this war of empires. In fact, the African war lasted even longer than the European one: the last German surrender was not until late November 1918. Only then did Lieutenant Colonel Paul von Lettow-Vorbeck, having led a dogged guerrilla resistance in East Africa, finally receive news of the **Armistice**. Most of the German colonies fell quickly – Togoland (modern Togo) within two weeks, South West Africa (modern Namibia) to South African forces in July 1915, and Kamerun (most of modern Cameroon) in February 1916. German East Africa (Rwanda, Urundi and most of present-day Tanzania) was a different matter. There African *Askari* soldiers fighting for Lettow-Vorbeck proved extremely loyal, perhaps because he believed, unusually, that 'the better man will always outwit the inferior, and the colour of his skin does not matter'. He was fêted as a German hero after the war, but his tenacious resistance also wreaked havoc on the lands he fought across. The white British (including South Africans and Rhodesians) employed Indian troops but were initially reluctant to arm many black Africans; for one thing, they were worried at the possibility of rebellion – and in Nyasaland a pastor, John Chilembwe, did foment a revolt, angered at Africans having 'to die for a cause that is not theirs'. But the British soon came to rely totally on tens of thousands of Africans coerced into carrying supplies in terrain where **horses** were decimated by the tetse-fly. One estimate is that 200,000 of the carriers died from disease and malnutrition. It was a shocking reflection of the conditions and official neglect. Eventually, much of the fighting, too, was borne by men of the indigenous King's African Rifles.

EH & AL

ALLIES

The original Allies in August 1914 were Britain, **France** and **Russia** – the members of the Triple **Entente** (and hence alternative designation: 'the Entente Powers'). They were joined later that month by **Japan**, Britain's ally since 1902, and **Serbia** and Montenegro. In May 1915 **Italy** joined the Allies, and the following year, in March and August respectively, so did Portugal and Romania. Tiny San Marino became the smallest Ally when it declared war on Austria-Hungary on 3 June 1915. In 1917 Greece, politically divided and with Allied troops already encamped along the **Salonika** Front, formally sided with the Allies. The **United States** declared war on Germany on 6 April 1917 but as an 'Associated Power' rather than an Ally, a distinctive status which it shared with **Belgium**. Eight Latin American countries also

declared war on Germany, although only Brazil made a
significant contribution – a naval one – to the Allied cause.
Many of these later arrivals had more of an eye on possible
political advantages than on fully engaging with the war effort.
In the Far East, Siam (modern Thailand) declared war on
Germany and Austria-Hungary on 22 July 1917 and sent a token
expeditionary force to the **Western Front**. Liberia, then one of
only two independent states in Africa, declared war the following
month, as did China, which was already making a significant
contribution in the shape of 140,000 men who undertook
non-combatant roles on the Western Front.

TC

AMIENS

The Battle of Amiens was launched by Australian, British and
Canadian troops of the British Fourth Army (with the support
of the French First Army) on 8 August 1918. As part of a
campaign orchestrated by Marshal **Foch**, it was strategically the
turning point for the British. It effectively began the Allies'
Hundred Days Offensive, which brought the war to an end,
and it provided a template in terms of the tactics that would
characterise those last months. Conversely, for the Germans, it
was memorably lamented by **Ludendorff** as 'the black day of
the German Army'. Building on the lessons learnt at **Cambrai** in
1917 and at Hamel in July 1918, the British and Imperial forces
exploited careful secrecy in the planning and surprise in the
tactics, as demonstrated in the short but extremely sharp artillery
bombardments – so very different to the two-week pounding
preceding the **Somme** campaign. The battle witnessed a large-
scale use of aircraft, as well as every tank the British had available
– over 550 of them. Two days later, with their objectives won and
having inflicted around 70,000 casualties on a stunned enemy,

the British halted the offensive as German reserves bolstered a
new defensive line. But it had been a significant and morale-
boosting Allied victory.

SR

ANZAC

'ANZAC' was the official acronym of the Australian and New
Zealand Army Corps, and 'Anzacs' was also used unofficially to
describe members of the Corps. The huge military contribution
made by both these British dominions was out of all proportion
to the size of their populations. Australia, with fewer than
5 million inhabitants, sent 322,000 men to serve overseas. Of
these, 280,000 became casualties, including almost 60,000 dead,
the highest rate of attrition suffered by any national army in the
war. New Zealand, with a population of 1.1 million, recruited
124,000 men for the Army, 100,000 of whom served overseas.
Over half of them – 58,000 – became casualties, including 17,000
dead. Anzacs fought on the **Western Front**, in Egypt and the
Middle East, but most famously at **Gallipoli**. There on 25 April
1915 – since dubbed 'Anzac Day' – both countries, it is said, found
their true national identities for the first time. Australian 'Diggers'
and New Zealand 'Kiwis' had an awesome reputation as fighters
among both friend and foe; the former earned sixty-four **Victoria
Crosses**, while the latter garnered eleven. Along with that went a
reputation (on the part of the Australians) for a 'resolute lack of
military etiquette', said to outrage many a British officer. But
their own British commander, General Sir William Birdwood,
held them in the highest esteem, while **Lloyd George** later
claimed that he even considered the most able Australian
commander – Lieutenant General John Monash – as a possible
replacement for **Haig** to lead the **BEF**.

TC

ARMISTICE

The war witnessed periodic armistices, but *the* Armistice was the one that came into effect at 11am on Monday 11 November 1918 between the **Allies** and their one remaining enemy, **Germany**. It ended four years of hostilities, brought an eerie calm to the battlefields and saw jubilation across the victorious nations; but for Germany it brought defeat and turmoil. The Germans had first approached US President **Wilson** for an armistice on the basis of his Fourteen Points peace programme at the beginning of October 1918. He made it clear that Germany would have to fulfil several conditions (including an end to **U-boat** warfare), and that no peace could be concluded with Germany's present rulers. A month went by, as the Allies' **Hundred Days Offensive** further depleted Germany's military strength. On 7 November, the Germans were finally instructed to send a delegation to meet with Allied Commander-in-Chief **Foch** in a railway carriage in the Forest of Compiègne, north-east of Paris. There the Armistice was drawn up and signed. The German delegation had neither room for manoeuvre nor the opportunity to properly confer with their government on the terms imposed. These included the evacuation of all German-occupied **France** and **Belgium** and the surrender of much military equipment (and all U-boats). On 9 November, one obstacle – the issue of the **Kaiser** – was resolved as he fled into exile. The Allied blockade remained in force, as Germany still struggled to feed itself. The Armistice initially ran for 36 days and was regularly renewed as the Treaty of **Versailles** was thrashed out.

TC

ARTILLERY

More casualties on the **Western Front** were inflicted by artillery – canons and the stubbier howitzers – than by any other type of weapon. It is true to say that artillery gained a new level of importance, even dominance, on the battlefield in 1914–1918, shattering nerves and bones alike, and churning up the terrain into pitted landscapes. The solidification of the Western Front into trench lines put a premium on the ability to destroy the enemy's fixed defences in advance of an assault. And in 1915–1916 artillery bombardments grew in size, intensity and duration, while the warring nations corralled their **munitions** industries into producing more shells. The war conferred fame on a number of field guns that became the armies' workhorses – the French *soixante-quinze* ('75), the British 18-pounder, or the German 77mm gun – and in 1918 the Germans were even shelling the French capital with their monstrously sized 'Paris Gun'. In 1917–1918, new artillery techniques – such as the rolling barrage (as infantry advanced) and sound ranging (for better targeting) – along with innovations such as new fuses and gas shells replaced the lengthy poundings. German experiments at Riga (September 1917) and British experiences at **Cambrai** (November 1917) now allowed armies to achieve surprise with brief, yet highly concentrated and disorientating, bombardments. Combined with the use of aircraft, tanks, and cleverer infantry tactics, artillery contributed greatly to breaking the tactical stalemate in 1918. It certainly accounted for the most lives lost on the battlefield.

SR

ARTISTS

Artistic responses to the war embraced artists established and new, male and female, and amateurs sketching on active service as well as officially accredited War Artists. Britain's War Artists' scheme was set up as part of the **propaganda** effort in 1916, and from 1917 the artists proliferated. They included the respected John Singer Sargent who, in his sixties, was too old for active service. He completed the epic *Gassed* in 1919, a response to scenes witnessed after mustard **gas** attacks. Artists on active service included the Vorticist Paul Nash, who served with the Artists' Rifles (as did his painter brother John), until wounded; Stanley Spencer, who worked for the Royal Army Medical Corps before signing up as an infantryman in **Salonika**; and Eric Kennington, invalided out of the Army in 1915, whose autobiographical *The Kensingtons at Laventie* articulated the exhaustion of ordinary soldiers amid the bitter cold. Numerous women artists were also active, on the **home front**: Flora Lion and Anna Airy were commissioned to paint factory scenes, with Airy – a contemporary of William Orpen, the painter of the proceedings at **Versailles** – working on canvasses from life in the (often dangerous) factories themselves. As the war went on, artists often acquired humility in the face of what they saw. In 1915, C R W Nevinson may have insisted: 'there is no beauty except in strife, no masterpiece without aggressiveness'; but he, and others, modified their views when confronted with the reality of suffering. There was, in short, no *typical* war artist, but rather a hugely varied body of work. Many of these are now held by **Imperial War Museums** (IWM).

KC

ASQUITH

Herbert Henry Asquith (1852–1928), a statesman described as having 'the head of a Dickensian character and the nature of a Roman', became Britain's Liberal prime minister in 1908. He weathered many political storms, including that over Home Rule in **Ireland**, before having to deal with the European crisis as war loomed. Then, and in the first few months of war, Asquith's handling of events was much admired. A top civil servant recalled later: 'I was very much impressed by his clear, orderly mind, his coolness, courage and decision, and his amazing powers on seizing on essentials.' But, as the war dragged on, Asquith's laid-back style of governing brought criticism and impatience, with the actress and socialite Lady Tree even asking him: 'Mr Asquith, do you take an interest in the war?' In May 1915, as the scandal over the **BEF**'s shortage of shells erupted and failure at **Gallipoli** loomed, he went through a severe emotional crisis. For one thing, the 28-year-old Venetia Stanley, with whom he was passionately in love, announced her engagement to one of his own colleagues. Distraught and distracted, Asquith – against his better judgment – formed a new coalition government with the Conservatives. He remained as prime minister for the next year-and-a-half, but the death on the **Somme** of his eldest son Raymond was a further blow to his strength and spirit. He was increasingly overshadowed by his more energetic, and wily, Liberal rival **Lloyd George**, who finally toppled him from the prime ministership in December 1916.

TC

ASSASSINATION

Archduke Franz Ferdinand (1863–1914) became heir to the throne of **Austria-Hungary** after the suicide of Crown Prince Rudolf at Mayerling in January 1889. But his fame stemmed not from his life, but from his death by assassination in June 1914 – the spark that inflamed Europe's tensions and caused its power blocs to collapse into war. As heir to his uncle Emperor Franz Joseph, who had no great liking for him, Franz Ferdinand took his duties very seriously and was particularly interested in military and naval affairs. Some historians see him as a liberal who, had he lived, would have proved an enlightened and reforming emperor. Others regard him as a dyed-in-the-wool reactionary, bent on retaining the old order. Although on the surface he certainly appeared unbending and unlovable, he was also a devoted husband and father, who had defied his uncle to marry the insufficiently aristocratic Czech Sophie Chotek. During their visit to Windsor in November 1913, King George V found the archducal couple both 'charming' and 'very pleasant'. Seven months later, their joint visit to the Bosnian capital of Sarajevo on 28 June 1914 was much less happy. This former Ottoman province had been annexed by Austria-Hungary in 1908, but it included many ethnic Serbs and was coveted by neighbouring Serbia. A group of young Bosnian nationalists, encouraged by Serbian Army officers, planned to kill the archduke that day. One conspirator failed – his bomb hit the wrong car – but later that morning Franz Ferdinand and Sophie were both fatally shot at close range by the 18-year-old Gavrilo Princip. The dying words attributed to the archduke, 'Sopherl, Sopherl, don't die. Stay alive for our children!', were in vain.

TC

AUSTRALIA *see* ANZAC

AUSTRIA-HUNGARY

Who caused the war? The question is still being debated, but the first *declaration* of war was by Austria-Hungary against Serbia, following the **assassination** of Archduke Franz Ferdinand. To the amazement of many, the ramshackle Austro-Hungarian Empire entered the war almost united. Mobilisation, in which orders were given in 15 languages, was completed without dissent, and the empire's 52 million citizens appeared to rally around their ageing emperor, Franz Joseph. But by November 1916, when Franz Joseph died, the picture was very different. War on three fronts – against **Serbia**, **Italy** and **Russia** – with huge losses had brought the empire near to military, political and economic collapse.

'Shackled to a corpse' came to describe **Germany**'s ill-balanced entanglement with its weaker neighbour. A poor harvest in 1914 and the Allied blockade created food shortages in Vienna and elsewhere; another bad one in 1916 brought near starvation to the Austrian capital. Despite this, the government failed to draw up a centralised food policy or to properly organise rationing. The bad winter of 1916–1917 brought industrial output to a virtual standstill, except for the tools needed to prosecute the war. The new Emperor Karl failed to enthuse his peoples, and all his efforts to shore up the monarchy and to obtain peace ultimately failed. January 1918 saw a cut in the flour ration, strikes and riots, and ominously President **Wilson**'s promise of 'autonomy for all the peoples of the Austrian Empire'. By the autumn of 1918, the empire was falling apart, with Czechoslovakia proclaiming independence at the end of October. An armistice was signed on 3 November and Karl abdicated eight days later.

TC

BACKS TO THE WALL *to* BRUSILOV

BACKS TO THE WALL

Once Russia was out of the war, an opportunity arose for Germany to throw its forces fully against the **Western Front**. **Ludendorff** now planned for a mighty blow against the Allies, before US troops had a chance to bolster them. This *Kaiserschlacht* – 'Kaiser's Battle' – was targeted particularly at the British forces, and the onslaught began with Operation 'Michael' (21 March 1918), which ravaged the British Fifth Army. On 9 April 1918, the Germans followed up with their Georgette offensive along a narrow front east of the River Lys, between Béthune and Armentières: its aim was to force the British out of the **Ypres** Salient and drive on to the Channel coast. The initial assault was directed against two Portuguese divisions, who broke under the weight of the attack. Tired and under-strength British units on either side of them had to retreat with heavy casualties, and the Germans advanced 4 miles on the first day. Such was the pressure, and so high were the stakes, that Field Marshal **Haig** issued on 11 April a 'special order of the day' to 'all ranks of the British Army in France and Flanders'. The normally undemonstrative commander-in-chief told his embattled men, 'Words fail me to express the admiration which I feel for the splendid resistance offered by all ranks'. He acknowledged that the troops were tired, but observed: 'Victory will belong to the side which holds out the longest.' But it was, he recognised, potentially the final act: 'There is no other course open to us but to fight it out. Every position must be held to the last man; there must be no retirement. With our backs to the wall and believing in the justice of our cause each one of us must fight on to the end. The safety of our homes and the Freedom of mankind alike depend upon the conduct of each one of us at this critical moment.' As it turned out, the darkest moment for the **BEF** turned out to be the prelude to the decisive Allied **Hundred Days Offensive**.

TC

BALFOUR DECLARATION

The 'Balfour Declaration' was a letter, written in November 1917 by British Foreign Secretary Arthur Balfour, which was made public in the press on 9 November. It was addressed to Baron Rothschild, an influential leader of Britain's Jewish community, and it appeared to signal British support of the Zionist (Jewish nationalist) claim for a Jewish homeland in Palestine – though without mentioning a timescale. It was hoped that these intimations would be supported by Jews in Britain and the United States, and possibly undermine the support of German Jews for their country's war effort: a sizeable 95,000 Jewish men served in the German Army. The Declaration was – along with the **Sykes–Picot** agreement – testament to British ambitions to mould the post-war Middle East. But already Arabs in **Palestine** had been fighting to throw off Turkish rule, with aspirations for their *own* independent state. It would take another war – and the Holocaust – before the creation of Israel, but the Balfour Declaration is credited (or blamed) as one of the key historical documents in the modern Arab–Israeli conflict.

GR

BARBED WIRE

Among the images that came to evoke the inhuman landscapes of trench warfare, the ubiquitous barbed wire is prominent. It was invented in the United States in 1867 and designed to be a cheap, simple and rapid way of erecting a cattle-proof barrier. It was first used by the military as a defensive weapon during the Spanish–American War of 1898. In the First World War, once the patterns of trench warfare had set in, barbed wire came into its own. From late 1914 defensive entanglements of wire were laid out in **no man's land** to protect **trenches**. The repairing of the wire – and the cutting of the enemy's – was an ongoing task for the British

Tommy, performed under the cover of darkness. Wiring parties would sneak out into no man's land and insert pickets into the ground: steel poles, with corkscrew-like bases, which could be twisted quietly. Along the shaft of each pole were four loops where the barbed wire could be attached. Having to navigate uncut enemy wire could spell disaster for infantry on the attack, and one reason for **artillery** bombardments was to destroy barbed wire. Vanquishing the wire, and creating corridors for the infantry behind, was also an express purpose of the new **tanks**.

PS

BEF

'BEF' is an acronym for the British Expeditionary Force, the original title for all the British (and Imperial) forces who fought in France and Flanders during the war. The term endured even after a more formal retitling of forces as the 'British Armies in France and Flanders'. The BEF was created after the Anglo-Boer War (1899–1902) and was designed to be a rapid mobilisation force, capable of dispatch to the Continent in the event of a German invasion of France. Yet this professional army was miniscule by comparison with the conscript armies of Germany, Russia and France. The initial force that left for France in mid-August 1914 was comprised of four infantry divisions and five brigades of cavalry, and included both Regulars and part-time Territorials. By mid-September, the BEF was still little more than 160,000 strong. Later that month, reinforcements from **India** began to land at Marseilles, and further divisions crossed the Channel by November. Even so, the BEF's size paled in comparison with the numerous conscripts that Germany could put in the field, such that the **Kaiser** famously dismissed the British forces as a 'contemptible little army'. But the insult became a badge of pride, and the BEF's soldiers of 1914 were always henceforth known as 'Old Contemptibles'. From those Old Contemptibles, through the inexperienced volunteers who suffered so greatly on the **Somme**, to the battle-hardened fighters who pressed home to victory at war's end, the BEF travelled a long journey between 1914 and 1918.

PS

BELGIUM

'Gallant Little Belgium', as it soon became known in Britain, was invaded by German troops in the early morning of 4 August 1914. Belgian neutrality had been guaranteed by all the great powers back in 1839, but the Germans hoped that they would have a free passage through the small kingdom in order to invade France. In the event the Belgians resisted and their 'Soldier King' Albert became one of the war's first heroes in the Allied camp. Over a million Belgian civilians fled the German advance, the majority finding refuge in Holland; but more than 300,000 escaped to Britain and France. Brussels was occupied on 20 August, Antwerp on 9 October, and apart from a small western enclave around **Ypres** and the River Yser the entire country was under German occupation. German rule was harsh from the start and although some stories of atrocities were exaggerated, many were true enough. Louvain was looted and torched, with scores of its citizens shot in reprisal for acts of resistance. In other places, hostages were shot or used as human shields. In Brussels, its Burgomaster (Lord Mayor) Adolphe Max was imprisoned and deported for acts of defiance. Around 120,000 other Belgians were deported to Germany as forced labourers. The remaining population suffered hardship, alleviated to some extent by the American Commission for Relief in Belgium, masterminded by the future president Herbert Hoover. Belgian forces continued to fight alongside the Allies, both in Europe and in **Africa**, suffering 93,000 total casualties, while 30,000 civilians perished.

TC

BLACKADDER

Set on the **Western Front** in 1917, the satirical BBC TV comedy series *Blackadder Goes Forth* (1989) has exerted a strong influence on popular impressions of the war. It focuses on the various ill-fated attempts of the world-weary Captain Edmund Blackadder to escape the **trenches** and evade the orders of the cheerfully homicidal General Melchett (played by Stephen Fry). He is variously aided, or hindered, by his second-in-command Lieutenant George (Hugh Laurie) and their batman Private Baldrick (Tony Robinson). The plots often involve a ludicrous 'cunning plan' devised by Baldrick, which is usually rejected in favour of Blackadder's own guile. Both tend to prove ineffective, because of general incompetence, a change in circumstances or a mishap. Written by Richard Curtis and Ben Elton, the series exuded a strongly critical, anti-war tone reminiscent of the **'lions led by donkeys'** school of thought and has irked many historians for not presenting a balanced picture. Against this one could say that satire has different purposes from history, and *Blackadder Goes Forth*'s subversiveness has echoes of the Tommies' own **trench journals**. The programme-makers were keen not to trivialise the massive loss of life, and in the series' most memorable, closing, scenes the comedy runs out as Blackadder, Baldrick and George do indeed 'go over the top' to meet their fate – having exhausted all possible options to avoid the 'final push'.

RLH

BLIGHTY

The term 'Blighty' was first used by British soldiers stationed in India during the 19th century. It derives from the Hindi word *Bilayati*, meaning 'foreign' or 'far away', and so the soldiers serving the Raj adopted it to refer to their homeland of Britain. By the First World War it had started to be used more widely in the British Army. Its uses extended, so that a Blighty wound was one serious enough to get the victim invalided back to Britain, but not so serious that it was life-threatening. Indeed, getting a Blighty wound was often considered desirable – a means to escape the trenches – and some soldiers sought one out. There were various methods to incur a Blighty (or 'Blightie') – from the straightforward, but illegal, shooting oneself in the foot, to poking a leg or hand above the trenches to draw sniper fire or perhaps even some stray shrapnel. Clearly, the risk had to be carefully judged.

PS

BLOCKADE *see* GERMANY; ROYAL NAVY; U-BOATS

BLOODY APRIL *see* RFC

BRITAIN *see* ASQUITH; CHURCHILL; HAIG; HOME FRONT; LLOYD GEORGE; SCRAP OF PAPER; *see also* the entries on individual theatres, campaigns, and other aspects of the fighting fronts and home fronts

BRITISH EXPEDITIONARY FORCE *see* BEF

BRUSILOV

Aleksei Brusilov (1853–1926) is regarded as Russia's most capable commander of the war. His south-west offensive of 1916 left **Austria-Hungary** impotent militarily on the **Eastern Front**. Where many Russian actions in the war resulted in heavy casualties for little gain, the Brusilov offensive was, by contrast, a rare success. Coming from a military family, by 1914 Brusilov had risen to the rank of general and was commanding the Russian Eighth Army in Galicia, which initially performed well against the Austrians; but he was forced to fall back with the rest of the Russian Army in 1915. In March 1916 Brusilov was promoted to command the entire south-west front, and he formulated an audacious plan to ease pressure on the Russian lines. He relied on careful preparation and surprise, and thus he avoided an obvious artillery bombardment or a discernible build-up of reserves, so that, as he put it, 'our offensive surpassed all hopes'. Spring 1916 proved to be the high point for Brusilov. Unfortunately, his fellow commanders were not as dynamic or as able in their sectors, and he had to dissipate his thrust in order to try and help Romania resist the **Central Powers**. As casualties rose and disappointment fed the rising discontent in Tsarist Russia, the Russian Army began to fall apart in mutiny and political disaffection. Following the Bolshevik Revolution of 1917, Brusilov followed many of his soldiers in joining the Red Army, until retiring in 1924. He considered that a strong Russia was a higher priority than any particular political loyalties.

RWR

CAMBRAI *to* CONSCRIPTION

CAMBRAI

Had the Battle of Cambrai (1917) been a football match, it might well be summed up as a game of two halves. It began with a heady British success against the heavily fortified **Hindenburg Line**, which was instantly lauded by the press and set church bells ringing across Britain. It ended, two weeks later, with almost no gains at a cost of nearly 45,000 casualties and an enquiry into what went wrong. The dawn attack on 20 November, by elements of the British Third Army under General Sir Julian Byng, had an experimental quality: a massive, but short, bombardment, which aided the element of surprise; the largest concentration of tanks sent into battle thus far; rolling barrages in front of the troops, as they followed behind the tanks; support from **aeroplanes**; and even an opportunity for cavalry to charge behind the lines. The Hindenburg Line was breached. Yet the British became bogged down attempting to capture the high ground of Bourlon Wood, as the fighting descended into the familiar attrition. A well-organised counter-offensive (30 November) by the German Second Army achieved its own surprise blow, aided by 'infiltration' techniques of lightly armed, fast-moving 'stormtrooper' infantry. Within five days, the British were dispossessed of their recent gains. Nevertheless, the battle showed that the Hindenburg Line was not invulnerable, and the tactics employed (by both sides) heralded much that would come to fruition in 1918. A year later, on 8–9 October 1918, the Second Battle of Cambrai saw the town swiftly isolated and then taken by British and Canadian forces, after another assault prefaced by a 'hurricane' bombardment.

SR

CAMOUFLAGE

The military use of camouflage grew out of the eighteenth- and nineteenth-century hunting traditions, where adopting the colours of nature enabled hunters to blend into the background and conceal their presence. By 1914 most of the armies at war had turned away from the peacock splendour of military tradition and adopted the principles of camouflage in their military uniforms – with the notable exception of the French, who doggedly stuck to their red trousers and blue greatcoats. The number of casualties they suffered in the first few weeks of war prompted a rapid rethink, and soon French soldiers were also kitted out in something more natural – 'horizon blue'. The Germans favoured field grey, while the British Army had already adopted khaki. As the war went on, camouflage of materials, equipment and positions became ever more sophisticated, especially given the new reality of aerial surveillance. The French formed teams of specialists – *camoufleurs*. In 1916 the British formed a camouflage section too and recruited highly talented artists to develop ways of disguising the presence of men and artillery. Increasingly, camouflage was becoming a matter of **deception**.

LW

CANADA

Canada entered the war in August 1914 as a self-governing Dominion within the British Empire. Its military forces were minuscule, but its government immediately offered to raise a force of 25,000 men to aid Britain. In the event, from a population of less than 7.5 million, 600,000 Canadians joined up, of whom 418,000 served overseas; more than 210,000 of them became casualties, including 56,500 dead. Another 28,000 Canadians served either in the Royal Canadian Navy, the **Royal Navy** or the **Royal Flying Corps**/Royal Naval Air Service, including the

ace 'Billy' Bishop VC. In addition, nearly 15,000 British citizens
resident in Canada returned to the mother country to enlist. In
Canadian shipyards there was an 850 per cent increase in capacity,
and by the **Armistice** over 900 small warships had been built by
them. Newfoundland was still a British colony. Out of its total
population of 250,000, nearly 10,000 served in the forces, a fifth
of them becoming fatalities fighting at **Gallipoli** and on the
Western Front. Newfoundland helped in other ways, too: 500
lumberjacks were dispatched to Scotland to aid British timber
production. Thousands of Canadian lumberjacks performed a
similar task in France. In Canada there remained strong divisions
between the English- and French-speaking populations over
controversial issues such as conscription. But the Dominion's
stalwart contribution and the successes of Canadian troops on the
battlefield (especially the totemic capture of Vimy Ridge in April
1917) contributed to a strong sense of nationhood, which ensured
Canada had a voice in the Imperial War Cabinet in London and
its own seat at the 1919 Paris Peace Conference.

TC

CAPORETTO *see* ITALY

CARIBBEAN

The British West Indies provided the regular West India
Regiment (WIR) – which took part in the fight against the
German colonies in West and East **Africa** – along with new
volunteers, spurred on by local newspapers' support for Britain.
But **Kitchener** opposed the raising of black Caribbean troops,
and it was only through King George V's intervention that
permission was given, in May 1915, for them to enlist. First they
had to undertake the long and difficult journey across the
Atlantic. In one instance, a troopship diverted via Halifax, Nova

Scotia, resulted in hundreds of Jamaican soldiers suffering amputations caused by frostbite. Once in France, the new British West Indies Regiment (BWIR) was employed in exhausting support duties – loading ammunition, digging trenches and laying telephone wires – but not allowed to fight. A poem of the day summed up their feelings: 'Stripped to the waist and sweated chest / Midday's reprieve brings much-needed rest / From trenches deep toward the sky. / Non-fighting troops and yet we die.' In **Palestine**, however, the BWIR *did* see front-line action. Indeed, General Allenby informed the governors of the West Indian colonies of 'the excellent conduct of the machine gun section of the BWIR during two successful raids on the Turkish trenches'. At the end of the war, the men of the BWIR were transferred to the British Army base in Taranto, Italy, until late 1919, where low pay and low-status work (such as lavatory cleaning) generated a mutiny, which was put down. For many of them, the war had broadened their horizons: 'Nothing we can do will alter the fact that the black man has begun to think and feel himself as good as the white' observed one Colonial Office civil servant. Nervous colonial authorities began encouraging demobbed Caribbean soldiers to emigrate.

SB

CAVELL

Relatively few individuals from the war strike a chord with the public over a hundred years later. One who does was the Norfolk-born nurse Edith Cavell who, in 1907, became Matron of Belgium's first training school for nurses – a decision that would lead to a kind of martyrdom. When war broke out, she formed a Red Cross hospital in Brussels and nursed wounded German and Belgian soldiers. Following the German occupation of the city, her institution was placed at the disposal of the invading army.

Despite being offered the chance to return to Britain, the principled and determined Cavell chose to remain with her nurses. But over the following year she became part of a network that helped some 200 Allied soldiers escape from German-occupied territory. On 5 August 1915, she was arrested by the German authorities along with five of her associates. Brought to trial on 7 October, she was executed four days later by firing squad on the orders of the Governor General of Brussels. The secretive manner of her execution and the sensational newspaper reports following the announcement of her death ensured that Cavell's fate generated shock and revulsion in Britain. Together with incidents such as the sinking of the *Lusitania* and the execution of a merchant seaman, Captain Charles Fryatt, her execution was amplified in Allied **propaganda** as evidence of the alleged inhumanity of the enemy.

AR

CENTRAL POWERS

Opposing the **Allies** in the war were the countries collectively titled the 'Central Powers'. **Germany** and **Austria-Hungary** were the two original members in August 1914; but **Italy**, their partner in the pre-war Triple Alliance, and Romania, a secret signatory to that alliance, declined to join them in war. At the end of October 1914, after its ships (donated by the German Navy) had bombarded Russia's Black Sea ports, **Turkey** became the third Central Power. On 14 November 1914 the Sultan proclaimed a *Jihad*, or holy war, hoping to foment revolt among the Muslim subjects of the empires of Britain, France and Russia. In October 1915, Bulgaria, under Tsar 'Foxy' Ferdinand, became the final recruit to the Central Powers and joined with the others in crushing Serbia. The next year all four Central Powers combined to attack and defeat Romania, and in late 1917 they met at

Brest-Litovsk to dictate peace terms to Lenin's new Bolshevik regime in Russia. From this high point, the alliance began to fall apart at the end of September 1918 when Bulgaria signed an armistice with the Allies. Turkey followed suit a month later, and then, on 3 November 1918, the crumbling Austro-Hungarian Empire signalled its own surrender, leaving Germany – always by far the most powerful of the group – isolated.

TC

CHRISTMAS TRUCE

One of the most amazing, but atypical, episodes of the war was the Christmas Truce of 1914. Since then, it has become the subject of much mythologising, and even at the time it seemed incredible that after four months of bitter fighting, 'war was absolutely forgotten' between the two sides for a few hours. The truce began in some areas late on 24 December. One officer wrote that 'When I got back to our trenches after dark on Christmas Eve, I found the Boches' trenches looking like the Thames on Henley Regatta night. They had got little Christmas trees burning all along the parapet.' From the German trenches, British troops heard carols and invocations shouted out: 'You English, why don't you come out?' The following day, British and German soldiers met in **no man's land** and exchanged gifts of cigars and cigarettes, took photographs and had impromptu kickabouts. Part of the day was devoted to burying the dead and to reinforcing **trenches** against the common enemy, flooding. British and German working parties shared hammers, mauls and other tools. 'They weren't half a bad lot, really', wrote one **Tommy**. Not all sectors of the British line observed the truce, though, and men were killed and wounded on Christmas Day. Fighting proper resumed on Boxing Day, and a British officer wrote: 'A hail of rifle and machine-gun fire swept the parapet. Hell was let loose again; it was Business as Usual.'

TC

CHURCHILL

Winston Churchill's career during 1914–1918 is overshadowed by his defining role in the Second World War. Yet he had a colourful and varied First World War career, which established a reputation for boldness and energy – and in the eyes of critics, rashness. In 1914 he was in **Asquith**'s Liberal Cabinet, holding civilian authority (from 1911) over the **Royal Navy** as First Lord of the Admiralty. He described these three years, which he spent modernising the Navy and keeping it the world's most powerful, as some of the happiest in his life. He also gave naval backing to the development of 'landships', which would become better known as **tanks**. But his eager advocacy of the disastrous attempt to force the Dardanelles Straits in March 1915 and the ensuing failure of the **Gallipoli** campaign precipitated his resignation from the Cabinet in November 1915 and a request for a posting to the **Western Front**. During the six months Churchill spent in Flanders, he led thirty-six forays into no man's land, and he raised morale by taking a keen interest in his men's personal welfare; he was also notably critical of the government's conduct of the war. He recorded his front-line experiences in letters to his wife Clementine – adding in requests for his favourite whisky and peach brandy. In July 1917, and with **Lloyd George** now prime minister, Churchill was back in the Cabinet, holding Lloyd George's old portfolio as Minister for Munitions until 1919.

SC

CONSCIENTIOUS OBJECTORS

When, after heated debate, Parliament passed the Military Service Act in January 1916, **conscription** became a fact of British life. But there was provision in the legislation for the exemption of those men with a 'conscientious objection' to bearing arms. Between March 1916 and the end of the war,

16,000 men registered as conscientious objectors. They included 6,000 'Absolutists', like the five sons of hatter George Arthur Dunn, who had a total objection to any form of war service, while the remainder were 'Alternativists' who, though they refused to fight, were prepared to accept substitute forms of service such as agricultural work. Over 2,000 tribunals were established to consider appeals on the grounds of conscientious objection and to appraise the sincerity of those like Howard Marten, who not only refused to fight but also objected 'to having one's life directed by an outside authority'. They were a diverse group, some impelled by religious scruple, such as Quakers and Jehovah's Witnesses, others by radical politics or other concerns. They could find themselves rubbing shoulders in one of the prisons, such as Dartmoor, that had been given over to wartime duty as work camps. Conscientious objectors were almost universally despised. Signs were displayed in many shops that 'conchies' would not be served, and there were several ugly incidents, as at Knutsford in 1918 when some were physically attacked. And even those people sympathetic to their cause could find them, as did Beatrice Webb, 'saliently conscious of their own righteousness with their claim of "we are the only ones whose eyes are open"'.

TC & EF

CONSCRIPTION

Following the outbreak of war, **Kitchener** had energetically raised his so-called 'New Armies' of volunteers. During the first year-and-a-half of the war, a staggering 2,675,149 men volunteered for the Army, and 547 service battalions were created by June 1916. But when the **recruitment** numbers began to slow, the National Registration Act of July 1915 determined all men of military age, and then the Derby Scheme asked men to 'attest' their willingness to serve either immediately or if asked to do so in the future – on the promise that all unmarried men would be selected first. Too few single men attested, and eventually Parliament resorted to legislation for conscription. With the Military Service Act (27 January 1916), compulsory military service was implemented from March, a first in British history. This initial Act covered eligible unmarried men (and widowers), aged between 18 and 41, who were not engaged in essential war work, or on whom others were not financially dependent. Other categories of exemption included ill health, what were judged to be *bona fide* claims from **conscientious objectors**, and working as a clergyman. And the scope was limited to mainland Britain, so it excluded **Ireland**. With a second Act a few months later, married men too were to be called up. Conscription was an uncomfortable, controversial measure, which went against British tradition; but it was accepted as a necessity by the vast majority.

CM

DECEPTION *to* DREADNOUGHTS

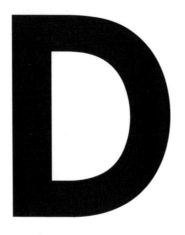

DECEPTION

As war progressed, **camouflage** as simple concealment was increasingly accompanied by attempts to deceive or confuse the enemy. A prime example is the 'Dazzle' technique of painting created by Lieutenant-Commander Norman Wilkinson, a marine painter before the war. Supposedly inspired by the plumage of Eider ducks, he argued that painting British vessels in bold shapes and high-contrast colours, with unusual angles and curves, could significantly dent the **U-boats**' ability to gauge a ship's outline, speed and direction of travel. He and his team of artists at the Royal Academy designed patterns and tested them on model ships viewed through a periscope. Although initially intended for merchant ships, Dazzle designs were later adopted by both the British and US navies. Meanwhile, on the **Western Front** various types of dummy items were created to hoodwink the enemy. Human heads made of *papier mâché* were raised above the parapet of a trench, to lure enemy sniper fire; the sharp-shooter, having given away his location, could then be targeted by counter-fire. Artificial hollow tree-trunks, resembling the blasted trees of the battlefield, were also created to serve as observation posts. The real tree would be chopped down quietly at night, to be replaced with its man-made equivalent concealing a soldier, perhaps equipped with field glasses. East Africa witnessed one of the more unusual examples of deception, as the wild 'zebra' population expanded – in reality, British **horses** and ponies painted in stripes to conceal their true identities.

NV

DESERTION

Rates of desertion in the First World War varied – both between armies, and within armies at different times. Individual regional and national loyalties among the forces of **Austria-Hungary** inevitably affected their cohesiveness, and the Italian Army suffered high desertion rates in spite of (or perhaps because of) draconian and often arbitrary punishments. The French Army experienced a crisis of morale in 1917, often described as a 'mutiny'. By contrast, the British rate of desertion, at about one man in every hundred, was low. Nevertheless, there is a popular impression of numerous soldiers wrongly convicted of cowardice or desertion suffering the ultimate fate: 'shot at dawn'. Execution was, of course, the most serious punishment available in military law. Of the 346 death sentences carried out by the British military, 266 were for desertion, 3 of the condemned being officers. But perhaps the most remarkable fact about British death sentences is that nearly 90 per cent of them were commuted, the majority by Field Marshal Sir Douglas **Haig** himself. Many deserters instead received custodial sentences – sometimes suspended, if the men were needed at the front. (An unwilling soldier was, presumably, better than no soldier at all). The notion that one weapon in a firing squad contained an empty or blank round, so that no one would have to carry the burden of knowingly firing the lethal shot, has been shown to be myth: any trained soldier would know what firing live ammunition would feel like.

NV

DIARIES

Diaries from the war years provide an invaluable primary source for understanding the conflict, recording the personal experiences of individuals from all kinds of backgrounds. The Documents and Sound Section of IWM's Department of Collections is home to many individual British and Commonwealth private diaries, while official diaries recording the service of military units are preserved at The National Archives. Civilian diaries reveal much about the way in which the war was experienced at home: the thoughts and beliefs of **conscientious objectors**, the monotony of work in the **munitions** factories, the pride felt by women allowed to undertake men's jobs for the first time – and much else besides. They commonly describe, too, the fears and hopes of the families whose loved ones were fighting overseas. Diaries of men and women on active service, on the other hand, can bring to life the daily realities of war through, for example, first-hand accounts of battles or descriptions of treating the wounded. While official documents tell the broad story of the war, it is important to remember the smaller, individual experiences, which help us to empathise with those involved. Keeping a diary was a straightforward practice for civilians, but for those subject to British military law it was a different matter: there were definite restrictions on what could legitimately be recorded. The General Routine Orders issued to the **BEF** listed 'forbidden information', including the names of locations, plans of future operations, references to the condition of troops or casualties, defensive works, criticisms of superiors, the effects of hostile fire and statements calculated to bring the Army into disrepute. Even mentioning the weather might reveal the condition of trenches in that particular sector, so was discouraged. Fortunately for later generations, many individuals chose to ignore the regulations, providing, in their private diaries, vital personal testimony of the First World War.

AR

DISEASE

Disease accompanied every army on active service, but the ravages of **artillery** and the **machine gun** on the Western Front generated something new: for the first time, troops experienced a higher death rate from combat than as a result of illness and disease. This was not the case in every theatre – disease claimed the greater proportion of lives at **Salonika**, in **Mesopotamia** and in **Africa**. Some theatres suffered distinctive medical problems; malaria was rampant in Salonika, while dysentery was endemic throughout the **Gallipoli** campaign; both, and local diseases, bedevilled the campaign in East Africa. On the **Western Front** the manure-laden soil infected wounds with gas gangrene, while 'trench foot' was an ever-present threat where men lived in bitterly cold, waterlogged trenches: rubbing feet with whale oil was recommended to prevent trench foot, but both complaints could lead to amputation. **Lice** caused 'trench fever', which presented with flu-like symptoms and was first noticed in 1915. Nervous complaints such as **shell shock** or 'barbed wire fever' in prison camps proliferated. Venereal diseases continued to be a major problem, with nearly 24,000 beds set aside for this in British military hospitals in 1918. That year also brought a cruel finale to the war in the shape of the influenza pandemic that swept the world over the next two years, causing the deaths of millions – often from the pneumonia that came in its wake – and which was partially accounted for by troop concentrations and movements, and by demobilisation at the war's end. Advances in **medicine** contributed to better survival rates, and they included widespread inoculation against disease. Nevertheless, if disease was not quite the killer it had been in previous wars, its effects lingered after the war had ended. In 1919 Britain's Ministry of Pensions awarded 63 per cent of its payments to those suffering the effects of disease, whereas wounds accounted for only 35 per cent (and **gas** poisoning for just 2 per cent).

SP

DORA

Many of the rules and regulations that governed the lives of the British people during the war were introduced as part of DORA

– the Defence of the Realm Act. DORA was, in August 1914, concerned chiefly with protecting military information and 'securing public safety'. But as the war progressed it was amended and extended until there was scarcely an area of British home-front life that was not in some way affected or controlled by its wide reach and scope. Drunkenness, perceived to be a threat to wartime efficiency, was tackled through limits on pub opening times and the introduction of lower-strength alcohol. Land needed for military sites could be requisitioned in the Act's name, and food supplies controlled to help eke out scarce resources. It effectively curtailed the freedom of the press, and suspicious activities, such as loitering near tunnels and bridges, were forbidden. Even whistling for taxis in London was banned. The restrictions became increasingly unpopular with the public, especially as the Act was not immediately repealed at the end of the war – and some of its provisions (notably the licensing laws for pubs) lasted decades. *Punch* magazine reflected this unhappiness, depicting DORA as a censorious old woman: the 'British lion' on which she is perched in one April 1919 cartoon laments, 'I am getting a bit tired of this lady. After all, I'm a lion, and not an ass.'

CW

DOGS

Dogs made a multifaceted contribution to the war serving with many of the armies, whether as messengers, 'ratters' (to catch rats), sentry dogs, scouter dogs or mascots. Many breeds were used, but the most popular were two German native breeds: Doberman Pinschers and German Shepherds, because of their good trainability, high intelligence and guard-dog capabilities. Their dark coats and agility also allowed them to access enemy territory and carry messages without detection. Terriers, though, were used as ratters. By 1918, Germany had 30,000 military dogs; Britain,

France and Belgium had over 20,000; and Italy 3,000. By contrast, the United States did not use many dogs, though one of the most decorated dogs in military history was American: 'Sergeant Stubby', a stray Boston terrier. He became the only dog to be promoted sergeant through combat.

LM

DREADNOUGHTS

The term 'dreadnought' lies at the heart of Anglo-German tensions in the years before the war. Launched in 1906, HMS *Dreadnought* was a battleship of such revolutionary design and power that she immediately surpassed all others; and 'dreadnought' became the general term for successive vessels of her kind. A key innovation was a uniform battery of large guns, which made for greater firepower, more straightforward targeting and simpler logistics. HMS *Dreadnought* was also the first warship to be powered solely by turbine engines, and her top speed of 21 knots was at least 2 knots faster than any of her contemporaries. For naval traditionalists, the new technology seeming to spell the end of an era. Nevertheless, the building of new dreadnoughts became the focus of a concerted arms race between Britain and Germany, as the latter attempted to challenge the **Royal Navy**'s maritime dominance. At the outbreak of the First World War, the United States, Russia, France, Japan, Austria-Hungary and Italy had all begun adding the larger and more heavily-armed classes of 'super dreadnoughts' to their fleets. The British *Revenge*-class ships carried 15-inch guns. (Two of these – from HMS *Ramillies* and HMS *Resolution* – are displayed outside the **Imperial War Museum**, London). Dreadnoughts became intimidating symbols of naval power; but ironically the desire of navies to protect these most valued of assets led to cautious, defensive strategies, with the only major sea battle of the war taking place at **Jutland**.

TO

EASTERN FRONT *to* ENTERTAINMENT

EASTERN FRONT

When **Russia** declared war on **Austria-Hungary** in support
of its ally **Serbia**, it heralded the start of the bloody campaign
of the Eastern Front. It involved the forces of **Germany**,
Austria-Hungary and later Bulgaria against those of **Russia**
(and for a while Romania), and it ranged over a long front
stretching from the Baltic to the Black Sea, with much of
the fighting taking place in what is now Poland and western
Ukraine. It turned out to be a war of greater movement than
its Western counterpart, fought across the region's wide open
spaces, forests, lakes and (in the south-west) mountain passes
and witnessing a succession of retreats and advances. It was a
campaign where cavalry could still sometimes exert its traditional
role. It was sometimes a war of trenches too, especially in local
engagements or when winter weather caused all sides to dig in.
The casualties were undoubtedly huge, often dwarfing those
on the **Western Front**; but the precise numbers are harder to
specify. Russia's initial invasion of Germany's East Prussia came
to a disastrous end at **Tannenberg** and the Masurian Lakes in
August and September 1914. The Russians had greater success
against Austria-Hungary, but in 1915 combined German and
Austro-Hungarian offensives forced the Russian armies into
a large tactical retreat. The most talented Russian general,
Brusilov, led an effective counter-offensive against Austria-
Hungary in 1916, but in the end – disabled by poor logistics,
bad leadership, low morale and domestic discontent – it
was the Russians who broke first. After the abdication of
Tsar Nicholas in February 1917, and then the toppling of
the Provisional government in the autumn, Russia's new
Bolshevik rulers were anxious to extricate the country from
war, even at the cost of the humiliating terms imposed by the
Central Powers in the Treaty of Brest-Litovsk (March 1918).

The Eastern Front was over, and Germany sought to transfer its full military weight to the West.

RWR

ENTENTE

Entente is a French word meaning 'understanding'. Because French was the traditional language of diplomacy it was applied to the agreements that Britain concluded with **France** in April 1904, and with **Russia** in August 1907. The three powers were then known as the 'Triple Entente' – and so 'Entente Powers' is often used as an alternative designation for the **Allies** during the war. The opposing bloc was the Triple Alliance of **Germany**, **Austria-Hungary** and **Italy** (with Romania as a secret partner). This immersion in strategic alliances was new for Britain. For much of the late nineteenth century, Britain had been in so-called 'splendid isolation'. But the Anglo-Boer War of 1899–1902, during which there had been calls for a 'European Combine' against Britain, demonstrated that the country's diplomatic isolation was far from splendid. Hence the search for friends, beginning with an alliance with Japan in 1902, based on a mutual distrust of Russia in Asia. A similar mutual concern about Germany led Britain to sink its differences and colonial disputes with France. Following a hugely successful diplomatic charm-offensive by King Edward VII, the Entente Cordiale was signed. It was then a relatively short step to a similar understanding with France's Russian ally, although that *entente* was never as cordial as the one with democratic France. On 5 September 1914, the three countries signed the Pact of London, in which they each pledged not to make a separate peace, a pledge broken by Russia's new Bolshevik regime in November 1917.

TC

ENTERTAINMENT

A key factor in maintaining morale among British troops on the **Western Front**, and in breaking the monotony of trench life, was the regular rotation of troops – between different trench lines and also out of the line, where they could experience something akin to normal social routines: drinks at a bar, a game of **football**, simply the chance to chew the fat, as well as organised sports days, shows and competitions, and for those that wanted it, peace and contemplation. Great significance was placed on the idea that recreational activities aided the convalescing process. For many, irreverence was the order of the day. **Songs** and communal renditions of parodied hymns were popular, for instance, 'When This Bloody War is Over' to the tune of 'Take It to the Lord in Prayer'. Highlights were the theatrical performances. By 1917, each British division had at least one concert party, whose often colourful sketches gave the troops a safe outlet for their grievances about food, conditions and superior officers. Female impersonators were particularly popular and very occasionally a star of the stage would make it out to the front to entertain the troops. The culture of music halls and end-of-the-pier shows also underpinned the *Wipers Times*, the **trench journal** produced by the 12th Battalion, Sherwood Foresters, with its playlets and fake theatrical announcements ('For one Week Only – Miss Minnie Werfer', punning on the German *Minenwerfer* mortar). On the **home front**, entertainment in wartime had other priorities. It provided the usual escape valves, but it also fulfilled a **propaganda** function; it was a method both for encouraging recruitment and of fundraising for the war effort and the Armed Forces charities.

KG

FILM *to* FRANCE

FILM

In 1914, the film industry was barely 20 years old, but viewers were already enjoying silent melodramas, epics such as D W Griffith's *Birth of a Nation*, and comedies, as well as short documentary films covering topics from mountaineering to manufacturing. During the war, cinema attendances increased substantially in Britain. And it was in these years that British expatriate Charlie Chaplin became a worldwide success, his onscreen Little Tramp persona – with iconic moustache, bowler hat and cane – entertaining audiences in Allied and neutral countries alike. His potency as a global star overcame some domestic British criticism that Chaplin had not joined up. In October 1918 he released his own comic slant on trench life in the successful *Shoulder Arms*. The war also spurred an interest in films that could cast some light on the unfolding events. Cinemas became vehicles for news and **propaganda**, and documentary films became more numerous, longer and more elaborate. The best-known examples are the War Office-commissioned *The Battle of the Somme*, released in 1916, and its follow-up showing tanks in action, *The Battle of Ancre*. Produced as a morale booster, *The Battle of the Somme* was hugely successful. It was shot – sometimes as events occurred, sometimes in reconstruction – by British Army cameramen Geoffrey Malins and John McDowell, and it provided a novel but sometimes shocking depiction of the realities of life and death on the **Western Front**. Millions flocked to see it, and some gasped at being brought so close to the disturbing action of the war. Today, it is preserved in IWM's collections.

RLH

FOCH

Ferdinand Foch (1851–1929) was France's leading soldier of the First World War, and he held the pre-eminent role of Allied supreme commander on the **Western Front** from April 1918. Foch had been a pre-war instructor at France's *École de Guerre* (War College), where he had impressed on his pupils the importance of thinking and acting 'offensively'. When war arrived, he played a prominent part in the early battles of 1914, especially the Battle of the **Marne**, and in October he was appointed commander of the French Northern Army Group. He was less successful during the battles of 1915 and 1916, and in December 1916 was removed from his post, only to be recalled in May the following year to become Chief of the General Staff. In autumn 1917 he won laurels for co-ordinating Anglo-French support for **Italy** following its disaster at Caporetto. He performed a similar task on the Western Front in 1918, where the initial successes of the German spring offensives showed the need of having one overall Allied commander to co-ordinate the fight-back of the **Hundred Days Offensive**. In November 1918 it was Foch who presented terms for an **Armistice** to the German delegation in the train carriage at Compiègne. Foch got on fairly well with Sir Douglas **Haig** and **Lloyd George**, but less well with US General Pershing; however, King Albert of the Belgians said admiringly of him, 'that man could make the dead stand up at fight'.

TC

FOOD *see* AUSTRIA-HUNGARY; GERMANY; RATIONING

FOOTBALL

The most famous football match of the war is, at the same time, the most difficult to verify: the Anglo-German game (or games) supposed to have occurred in **no man's land** as part of the **Christmas Truce**. Any opportunity to play football, and escape the confines of the trenches, was certainly grabbed by Tommies. But the history of the sport in 1914–1918 also provides an interesting sidelight on the war's priorities and the recruitment of **Pals** battalions. When war broke out, many professional sports, such as cricket, ceased; but the Football League continued, attracting criticism for putting footballers' careers before the war effort. Indeed, feelings ran so high that it was suggested that King George V revoke his patronage of the Football Association. In reply to this outcry one politician, Joynson Hicks, formed the first Footballers Battalion (17th Middlesex) in December 1914; it was followed by a second (23rd Middlesex) in May 1915. Amateur footballers and fans joined the battalions too, to fight alongside their professional icons, which they did at a host of now-resonant locations, such as Delville Wood, Guillemont, **Cambrai**, **Messines**, Pilckem Ridge and the Menin Road. One professional footballer, Walter Tull of Northampton Town FC, became the first black man to become an officer in the British Army. Another player (for Wolverhampton Wanderers), Donald Simpson Bell, was awarded the **Victoria Cross** for clearing a German machine gun post under heavy fire, only to die five days later.

DF

FOURTEEN POINTS *see* ARMISTICE; WILSON; VERSAILLES

FRANCE

Outside France, the huge contribution that the country made to the Allied victory in 1918 is often overlooked. Over 8.3 million men served in the French Army, including 475,000 from France's overseas empire. France suffered almost 50 per cent more casualties than the British and Imperial forces did, an estimated 6.16 million by November 1918, which included 1.3 million dead.

For France, early hopes of successful offensives to retake Alsace and Lorraine from Germany gave way to a war to evict the German invaders, with Paris itself under threat on two occasions. Yet French troops fought not only on the **Western Front** (where it was accepted that the Allied supreme commander would be a Frenchman), but also in **Italy**, at **Gallipoli** and **Salonika**, and in **Africa** and **Palestine**. France's Navy played a key role, especially in the Mediterranean, and by the time of the **Armistice** the French Air Service numbered 127,630 officers and men and 3,222 machines. France's 'finest hour' came with the heroic defence of **Verdun** in 1916; but the following year saw mutiny in the Army and defeatism at home. Morale was to a great extent restored by General **Pétain**, from May 1917, and by **Clemenceau** after he became premier in November 1917. Clemenceau galvanised the French people with his words 'My home policy: I wage war. My foreign policy: I wage war. All the time I wage war', earning himself the title 'Father of Victory'. But that victory came at a huge cost , and not only in French lives. Seven million acres of northern France had been devastated, over 250,000 buildings totally destroyed and a further 350,000 severely damaged. Industrial production was down to 60 per cent of its pre-war level, and the franc had depreciated by 15 per cent. The war left deep physical and psychological scars on France, which played their part in the Fall of France in June 1940.

TC

GALLIPOLI *to* GERMANY

GALLIPOLI

The Gallipoli campaign was an ill-conceived attempt in 1915 to wrest the Dardanelles Straits from **Turkey**. It achieved notoriety as a costly, dismal failure, though it established a reputation for courage and endurance on the part of the **ANZAC** forces taking part. The aims included trying to reopen the sea routes to Russia's Black Sea ports (and potentially knocking Turkey out of the war through the capture of Constantinople). It was also planned as a naval operation: **Churchill**, as First Lord of the Admiralty, keenly advocated it. Thus, on 18 March 1915 a fleet of British and French warships attempted to force their way through the Dardanelles, only to meet accurate shell fire from Turkish shore batteries and an unexpectedly large number of mines. An amphibious invasion of the Gallipoli peninsula to the north, intended to silence the Turkish guns, merely ushered in eight months of trench warfare. Stiff Turkish resistance, inhospitable terrain, the sometimes appalling extremes of heat and cold, and rampant **disease** (including dysentery and malaria) made lives miserable. After a visit by **Kitchener** to see for himself, the decision was made to withdraw in late 1915. The eventual evacuation in the face of the enemy proceeded, ironically, without a hitch. The Allied victims of the whole enterprise included not only almost 300,000 casualties (around 60,000 of them dead), but also **Asquith**'s Liberal government, now forced into coalition, and Churchill himself, now demoted. In Turkey, the successful defence of Gallipoli at a cost of perhaps 250,000 casualties (65,000 killed) is seen as a defining historical moment: Mustafa Kemal, better known as 'Atatürk', was a divisional commander there, and it was he who founded the modern Turkish republic. Today Gallipoli also has huge national importance in Australia and New Zealand. The date of the first landings, 25 April, is 'Anzac Day', on which both nations continue to commemorate their casualties in all conflicts.

RR

GAS

Lines of gassed soldiers, their eyes bandaged, have become enduring images of the war. Gas inspired not only John Singer Sargent's epic painting *Gassed* (1919) but also Wilfred Owen's visceral poem 'Dulce et Decorum Est' with its evocations of men 'bent double' with their 'froth-corrupted lungs'. The introduction of poison gas seemed to herald a new low in warfare. In 1914, French and German troops fired specially designed gas-filled projectiles at each other – rifle grenades and artillery shells – but these contained merely tear gas. But on the **Eastern Front** the German military, and its scientists, began experimenting with something more sinister, and the first lethal deployment of gas on the **Western Front** occurred on 22 April 1915, in the Second Battle of **Ypres**. The Germans opened multiple canisters containing chlorine gas along their front lines, and with a favourable wind the result was disarray among the opposing French and North Africans, causing mass withdrawals and heavy casualties. But soon gas, of various kinds, became part of the arsenal on all sides. It also sparked hurried developments in personal protection. These started out as simple mouth guards – such as cotton pads or sanitary towels dipped in bicarbonate of soda or urine – and eye goggles. Eventually, they evolved into the gas helmet and, later, the much more sophisticated box respirator. However, even the box respirator was of little value against mustard gas, which could be absorbed into the body following contact with unprotected skin. Gas could be unpredictable and sometimes – with the wrong wind direction – as disruptive to those launching it as to the intended targets, as the British discovered at the Battle of Loos on 25 September 1915. In the end, only 2 per cent of all gas casualties became fatalities. But gas was universally hated, and the psychological impact was overwhelming – as it remains today whenever states are accused of using poison gas.

PWD

GERMANY

The Germans began the war with high hopes of a speedy victory. During the first week of August 1914, the **Kaiser** told departing troops: 'You will be home before the leaves have fallen from the trees'. But the optimism soon evaporated, and Germany, as with the other warring nations, began preparations for a long war. Nevertheless, there was a great upsurge in patriotism, with citizens subscribing to war loans and surrendering their precious metals. Hatred for Britain was encouraged and 'God punish England' became the slogan of many Germans. Life, though, became increasingly difficult over the war years. Dancing in public was banned and so too was ragtime music. Almost from the start, the Allied naval blockade began to bite, and despite the government's best efforts to control the distribution of consumer goods, severe shortages occurred. Clothes were rationed and often made of *ersatz* (substitute) materials – indeed, much in German life became a poor substitute for the real thing. By the early summer of 1915, food was becoming scarce and expensive, prices having increased by 65 per cent since July 1914. Rationing was introduced but was badly handled, and in one Silesian city troops had to be called out to control rioting *Hausfrauen*. There was considerable industrial unrest too. The harsh winter of 1916–1917 led to a major food crisis, and some estimates put civilian deaths from malnutrition at 700,000 by 1918. At the same time the **Hindenburg** Programme to mobilise the home front was introduced. But long before the **Armistice**, in one description, 'German patriotism had all but dissolved. A poorly clothed, poorly fed civilian population had no desire to prolong the war.'

November 1918 brought an end to hostilities before any of the fighting reached German soil; but it also brought defeat, revolution, turmoil on the streets, a continued Allied blockade, occupation armies in the Rhineland, and in 1919 all the indignities of the Treaty of **Versailles**.

TC & MS

HAIG *to* HUNDRED DAYS OFFENSIVE

HAIG

The taciturn Scottish soldier, Sir Douglas Haig (1861–1928), has been and remains a highly controversial figure, with opinion divided between hagiography and acute hostility. Having been at the centre of the reforms of the British Army following the Anglo-Boer War of 1899–1902, this former cavalry officer is often seen as representing the supposedly ineffective and costly British performance in France and Belgium from 1914. He began by commanding I Corps in 1914, then the First Army in 1915, before – following the resignation of Sir John French – leading the **BEF** (as 'Commander-in-Chief of the British Armies in France') in 1915–1918. As such, no British general was more associated with the **Western Front**. Decades later, Haig came to epitomise a popular idea of inept bungling (the **'lions led by donkeys'** view), as caricatured by David Low's cartoon 'Colonel Blimp'. He suffered, too, from a poor relationship with **Lloyd George**, who never liked or trusted him and who was highly critical in his memoirs. In recent years a more nuanced picture has emerged. Although rightly blamed for costly failures in 1915–1917 – the battles of Loos, the **Somme** and **Passchendaele** – these are placed in the perspective of a 'learning curve' along which all generals were travelling as they sought a way out of the stalemate of trench warfare; and Haig deserves more credit for the gradual improvement and successes of 1917–1918, which finally led to victory, as well as for his steadfastness when crisis hit (*see* **Backs to the Wall**). Modern historians have also emphasised the difficulties of moulding an army that was essentially a colonial police force prior to 1914 into a much larger force, of volunteers and conscripts, capable of defeating the Germans. Haig's most public legacy, though, looms large every November. Post-war, he devoted much of his energy to welfare for veterans, and his Earl Haig Fund inaugurated the modern **Poppy** Appeal.

SR

HINDENBURG

As a young man, Paul von Hindenburg (1847–1934) had fought in the Franco-Prussian War and was present when Prussian Chancellor Bismarck proclaimed the new German Empire at Versailles in January 1871. He had retired in 1911, but in August 1914 was recalled and ordered to halt the Russian invasion of East Prussia. There, due mainly to the brilliant staff work of his subordinates **Ludendorff** and Max Hoffmann, he could claim decisive victories at **Tannenberg** and the Masurian Lakes. Hindenburg now became the idol of Germany, soon eclipsing the **Kaiser** himself. He was promoted field marshal and given command of all the **Eastern Front**. Despite achieving a number of victories, he was unable to knock Russia out of the war. Nevertheless, in August 1916 he became Chief of the General Staff, with Ludendorff as his deputy. For the rest of the war the two men exercised a virtual dictatorship over Germany, effectively conducting its military *and* civil policy. Although Ludendorff was the driving force, it was Hindenburg's enormous prestige that counted with the public. In the tense days of early November 1918, with defeat looming, Hindenburg successfully advised the **Kaiser** to abdicate so that an **Armistice** could be agreed. There were Allied calls for Hindenburg's prosecution as a war criminal, but once again he went into retirement, only to re-emerge in 1925 when he was elected Germany's president. On 30 January 1933, he appointed Hitler as chancellor. As Nazi stormtroopers paraded through Berlin, Hindenburg, now suffering from dementia, is said to have remarked: 'I never knew we took so many Russian prisoners.'

TC

HINDENBURG LINE

During March and April 1917, German forces on the **Western Front** withdrew to a series of defensive zones running from Arras to Laon, which they called the *Siegfriedstellung* (Siegfried Line), but which the British knew as the Hindenburg Line, after Germany's military supremo Paul von **Hindenburg**. Construction began in the autumn of 1916, and during the Germans' withdrawal to it they adopted a scorched-earth policy, laying waste to the countryside, poisoning wells and setting up many booby traps for the Allies. The Germans had, in effect, straightened an awkward bulge in their front line, and so now defended a front that was almost 27 miles (42km) shorter than before, allowing them to release over 10 divisions for service elsewhere. And the new Line's defences were formidable. Its main battle zone consisted of artfully sited concrete machine-gun emplacements and trenches dug in a zig-zag pattern, which allowed the **machine guns** to sweep the angles. Thick belts of **barbed wire** proliferated. Nevertheless, part of the Hindenburg Line was breached by British troops during the Arras offensive (spring 1917) and again at **Cambrai** (November 1917), proving that it was not impregnable. In 1918 the Line was decisively broken by the British, between 12 September and 9 October. South African officer Deneys Reitz wrote: 'On a fourteen mile front […] they had blasted through the Hindenburg Line into the open country beyond, and from then on the evil of the old trench warfare was a thing of the past.'

TC

HOME FRONT

The First World War has often been described as the first example of **total war**, understandable only by taking into account the resilience – or otherwise – of entire populations at home.

In his *War Memoirs*, Lloyd George wrote: 'Armies might gain successes or meet with reverses; but once great nations had become thus mobilised for war, they could not be forced to surrender unless their home front broke down.' As he observed, 'That happened to Russia. In the end it befell […] Germany.' To a greater or lesser extent, all the warring nations experienced the same conditions on the home front. In Britain, civilians in towns and cities came under air attack from **Zeppelins** and **aeroplanes**, while Parisians were bombarded by long-range artillery. The Allied blockade brought about starvation in **Germany** and **Austria-Hungary**, and the **U-boat** campaign reduced Britain's food stocks to dangerously low levels. Shortages and **rationing** of food, clothes and other commodities became widespread. And the state intervened in the everyday lives of citizens to an extent unimaginable before 1914. **Women** took on jobs previously seen as male preserves (most famously as **munitionettes**), men adapted existing skills to wartime purposes, and even schoolchildren were mobilised to collect salvage or help with the harvests. (France also witnessed an influx of men from its colonies and beyond to perform much-needed labour in the factories and behind the front line, but this development also had a destabilising social effect.) 'Super patriots,' equipped with white feathers, harried young men not in uniform to join the colours. Enemy aliens were rounded up and interned. And hatred for the enemy, stoked by **propaganda**, was more widespread and more virulent than in any previous war. For the Allies, anything at home that had a Germanic whiff became suspect. In the United States, *Sauerkraut* was renamed 'Liberty Cabbage', while in Effingham, Surrey, the Blucher hotel's image problem was solved by its reinvention as the 'Sir Douglas Haig'. Even the British royal family required a rebrand, from 'Saxe-Coburg-Gotha' to 'Windsor'.

TC

HORSES

Although some theatres of war, such as **Palestine**, witnessed cavalry tactics of the kind that the nineteenth century would have understood, on the **Western Front** the age of the **machine gun**, **artillery** and **trenches** changed all that. But if the cavalry were left in the wings, waiting to exploit that elusive breakthrough, between 1914 and 1917 the British Army's complement of horses and mules still rose from around 23,000 to over 1 million. The animals remained absolutely vital for moving things, and people, around. They dragged field guns, hauled ammunition wagons, carried food and other supplies, and ferried the wounded to be treated in field hospitals and the dead to be buried. So many horses also generated a huge logistical exercise to keep them fed, watered and well. Britain imported horses and mules from all over the world. At home, firms sold horses to the Army, but the War Office also requisitioned horses from civilians. Patriotism must have been sorely tested as domestic animals were examined, commandeered and dispatched to war, never to be heard of again. In one touching note to **Kitchener**, schoolgirl Freda Hewlett pleaded for her pony Betty to be saved, as her family had already given up two horses: Betty's reprieve arrived the next day. (The correspondence survives in IWM's collections). Conditions were severe for horses at the front: killed by artillery, injured by **gas**, and even drowning in the boggy Flanders mud – not to mention the ravages of skin disorders and other ailments. Hundreds of thousands of horses died, but many more were treated at the increasingly sophisticated veterinary hospitals and sent back to the front. With war's end, the number of military horses was out of all proportion to need. Many came to an ignominious end, sold off for horsemeat.

SH

HUN

War generates easy stereotypes of the enemy. In 1914–1918, the Germans were sometimes 'Fritz' or 'the Bo(s)che', but the most pointed designation was 'the Hun'. In August and September 1914, almost as soon as stories began to appear alleging German atrocities against Belgian and French civilians and cities, the word 'Hun' was being used to describe the perpetrators. Its overt association was with the feared fifth-century Attila, whose Hunnic Empire (including the lands of Germany and Austria-Hungary) was threatening the declining Roman Empire and the Christian Franks in France. More immediately, in 1900 the **Kaiser** had himself likened German retribution to that of Attila, as a response to the violence unleashed against Germans (and other Europeans) by the Chinese nationalist 'Boxer' sect. He declared: 'Just as the Huns, a thousand years ago under the leadership of Attila, gained a reputation by virtue of which they still live in historical tradition, so may the name of Germany become known in such a manner in China, that no Chinese will ever again dare to look askance at a German.' It was an unfortunate comparison. In August 1914, Rudyard Kipling warned in a patriotic poem that the 'The Hun is at the Gate!' After a false report of the destruction of Reims Cathedral later that year, readers of *The Times* were informed that the scene of destruction 'is hallowed ground to the modern Attila and to every Hun'. Increasingly, 'Hun' came to be favoured by British (and later American) recruitment and **propaganda** campaigns. The word would have a long and potent life.

TC

HUNDRED DAYS OFFENSIVE

The **Western Front** has – not unfairly – been associated with stalemate, in which the periodic convulsions of offensives moved the front lines only fractionally. In 1918, this sense of stagnation changed, first with the German offensives from March, and then with the decisive Allied counter-thrusts that came to be collectively titled the Hundred Days' Offensive. The German attacks had, by July 1918, been successfully resisted. Now, under the overall co-ordination of **Foch**, all along the Western Front Allied armies mounted their own offensives. The proportionally large British and Imperial contribution began on 8 August 1918 with the Battle of **Amiens**. Field-Marshal **Haig** switched his attacks from sector to sector, allowing his troops to recover and regroup between assaults. The separate British armies advanced parallel to one another, providing mutual support. The Germans found themselves constantly stretched and off-balance by the Allies' attacks, with the dwindling German reserves pulled hither and thither. The Allies successfully employed short, sharp bombardments and rolling barrages that followed troops as they advanced, as well as adopting combined-arms tactics embracing **tanks**, infiltration troops and **aeroplanes**. The pace rarely let up, and – to take one example – between 26 August and 11 November the British First Army fought from Arras back to where it began its war in 1914: **Mons**. Meanwhile, US forces were pushing up through the Argonne Forest and lining up with the French, who were advancing in several sectors, and Belgian forces were making significant inroads back into their country. A crucial point was reached in September 1918, in the breaking of the German **Hindenburg Line**, and by October the spectre of the Allies pressing on and into Germany itself made German politicians and generals realise that they had no choice but to seek terms. Tactically, the painful military lessons and techniques learnt after 1916 had ultimately provided the tools for victory in 1918.

SR

IMPERIAL WAR MUSEUM
to ITALY

IMPERIAL WAR MUSEUM

Such was the unprecedented scale and loss of the First World War, it was felt necessary to establish an institution to record and interpret the conflict even as it was going on. Thus the National War Museum was founded on 5 March 1917, with the intention of collecting and displaying material as a record of both civilian and military experiences, and to commemorate the sacrifices of all sections of society. Committees got to work on gathering artefacts, from armaments to women's clothing. In 1918 the organisation was renamed the Imperial War Museum – from the outset, it aspired to represent the contribution of the wider British Empire too. Its aim was not to be jingoistic, nor was it to be a memorial in the manner of the later Cenotaph or Menin Gate. Rather, as the Librarian of the day stated, 'the visitor […] will discover in the Museum no attempt to glorify war nor to emphasise victory over the enemy. People will find here what war means and for this reason the Museum will […] play its part in promoting the cause of peace.' The Imperial War Museum opened at the Crystal Palace on 9 June 1920, and it received an estimated 3 million visitors before 1924. It later moved to South Kensington before arriving at its current Lambeth location, site of the former Bethlem Royal Hospital ('Bedlam') in July 1936. Now known as IWM (Imperial War Museums), today the organisation exists across five branches nationally and its collections cover conflicts from 1914 right up to the present day. IWM's collections include visual and written responses to war, by way of major collections of **art, photography, film, diaries, letters** and audio-visual resources. IWM London, based in Lambeth, has recently undergone a major transformation – creating new, larger galleries to tell the story of the First World War in time for the centenary of 1914, as well a new atrium to display some of the collection's iconic objects.

HB

INDIA

In 1914 the Indian Army comprised 240,000 men, but war saw numbers swell with volunteers to 1.5 million, of which around two-thirds served overseas in Britain's global war. It had already become clear, in summer 1914, that Britain's own small army would be severely outnumbered by Germany's in the event of war. In this climate, Indian Army men were sent to bolster the British effort in Europe. Troops from several parts of the subcontinent were mobilised four days after war was declared, and by November 1914 no less than one-third of the 'British' forces on the **Western Front** comprised men of the Indian Expeditionary Force. Circumstances meant they fought not as a single army, but in units alongside British soldiers, sharing the hardships and dangers of the First Battle of **Ypres**, and they went on to play a crucial Western Front role over the next year, notably at the Battle of Neuve Chapelle (March 1915). Military authorities were generally punctilious in enabling different Indian cultural and religious practices, including dietary needs and burial arrangements – lessons learned after the Indian Mutiny in 1857. For the sick and wounded, Brighton's Royal Pavilion – deemed to be the most Indian-looking building in England – was turned into a highly publicised 'show' hospital, partly in the hope that recuperating men would compose enthusiastic letters home about their treatment. From December 1914 sightseeing tours even took convalescing Indians around London's landmarks. But in France and Belgium, **trenches**, industrial-scale warfare, losses and language differences also made for shocks and dislocations, as did the harsh winter of 1914–1915 for those soldiers still kitted out in their summer uniforms. There remained, too, the numerous prejudices of the day. By Anglo-French agreement, Muslim soldiers were allowed to marry French women, but Hindus were not; and the British Army council attempted to stop white nurses administering to Indian men. German propagandists railed at the use of non-white colonial troops against white Europeans, associating dark skin with 'savagery'. The Indian troops' own letters – many composed with the help of scribes – tell vividly of the men's diverse experiences through it all. (The letters have mostly vanished, but censorship transcripts of some survive). In 1915, with the arrival of Kitchener's recruits, most Indian troops left Europe, the bulk for **Mesopotamia** (which saw the largest Indian commitment of the war). The Indian Army also served at **Gallipoli**, in Egypt, **Palestine** and East **Africa**, and garnered no less than twelve **Victoria Crosses** in the conflict.

EH & AL

IRELAND

Ireland's history in the First World War left a difficult legacy. On the one hand, Irish men and women responded eagerly to calls to defend freedom in Europe, and tens of thousands of Irishmen volunteered for military service. On the other hand, some nationalists saw the war as an opportunity to throw off British rule, and by 1918 Ireland was more polarised than ever along political and religious lines. Arguably, though, the outbreak of war averted an earlier crisis. In 1912 Britain's Liberal government proposed Home Rule – self-government in Ireland, based in Dublin. But Unionists, eager to preserve British rule, were dismayed, banding together to sign the so-called Ulster Covenant. At the same time, an Irish identity that looked to Gaelic traditions was reinforcing the growing frustration among militant nationalists. By 1914, paramilitaries on both sides were gathering arms, and conflict seemed likely. But international events intervened, Home Rule plans were suspended and mainstream politicians on both sides urged Irishmen to fight the **Central Powers** under a British flag. Over 200,000 of them responded, serving in places such as **Gallipoli** and on the **Somme**. The militant nationalist insurrection that shook (mainly) Dublin in the 1916 Easter Rising was always likely to fail – it was hastily organised, the German-supplied weapons were intercepted, and the rebel leaders realised their actions were largely symbolic. But the execution of 16 leaders by firing squad fuelled resentment of British rule. In the General Election of 1918, the more uncompromising nationalists of Sinn Fein displaced most of the moderate nationalists: they then rejected their seats at Westminster, instead declaring an independent Irish Republic with a new parliament in Dublin. The scene was set for a war of independence that would lead to partition of the island – a compromise that created its own problems for the future.

RD

ITALY

When Italy entered the war in 1915, the country sided with the **Allies** – to the contempt of **Germany** and **Austria-Hungary**, its partners in the pre-war Triple Alliance. Both sides had sought to woo Italy, and Italian opinion was divided. Ultimately, Britain and **France** made the best offer; and besides, Italian aspirations were to regain historic territory – *Italia Irredenta* (Unredeemed Italy) – in the north-east, which lay within the Austro-Hungarian Empire and would not be given up willingly. Also spurred on by ambitions of becoming a major Mediterranean power, Italy signed the secret Treaty of London in April 1915, and declared war in May – at first only on Austria-Hungary. Italy's ill-equipped conscript army, led by General Luigi Cadorna, launched numerous offensives – the Battles of the Isonzo – for two years against well-entrenched Austro-Hungarian positions, with limited gains and high casualties on both sides. Much of this was unforgiving attritional mountain warfare, bringing its own challenges of weather, terrain and logistics. Then, in late 1917 at the Battle of Caporetto (also known as the Twelfth Battle of the Isonzo), the Italians were pushed back 70 miles under a combined Austro-Hungarian and German assault, bringing them near to collapse until they steadied the line. A change of command, fresh supplies and an influx of British and French troops restored morale. A new Italian offensive was not, though, launched until October 1918 – and by this stage it was against weakened and demoralised Austro-Hungarian forces, who collapsed and surrendered in vast numbers. By 3 November, Italy and Austria-Hungary had agreed an armistice. Despite victory and a high price in casualties and war debt, Italy was sidelined by Britain, France and the **United States** at the Paris Peace Conference of 1919. A key issue was the failure to win the port of Fiume – although it was not originally a war aim – and Vittorio Orlando, the Italian prime minister, walked out of the discussions in tears. In the years to follow, Mussolini and the Fascists exploited Italian dissatisfaction with a 'mutilated peace' to their advantage.

JV

JAPAN *to* JUTLAND

JAPAN

Japan's role in the war is one of the lesser known stories of the conflict. Already a maritime power, Japan declared war on Germany in August 1914, honouring its 1902 alliance with Britain. There was self-interest at work too: easy pickings in the shape of some German colonial possessions, and Japan saw an opportunity to obtain leverage in asserting other regional rights. Relatively swiftly, Japanese soldiers and ships (with some British support) moved to conquer Germany's military base on Chinese soil, at Tsingtao, though the ships of the German East Asiatic Squadron had escaped. During this action, aircraft from the *Wakamiya* carried out the world's first successful carrier air raid by sinking a German minelayer. Japanese forces also seized some of Germany's Pacific island possessions, to which the Allies did not object. That seemed to be the end of Japan's war, but in fact the Imperial Japanese Navy continued to take part in hundreds of Mediterranean convoys, with one ship, the *Sakaki*, sustaining heavy casualties as a result of a torpedo strike in 1917. In 1915 Japan issued its 'Twenty-One Demands', which called for the acknowledgement of Japanese rights in China. They were eventually agreed to, but controversial clauses requiring the appointment of Japanese advisors to Chinese government departments were dropped because of Western objections. International pressure once again thwarted Japanese ambitions at the Paris Peace Conference of 1919 – where Japan had an equal vote as a victorious ally – with particular opposition from Australia to the proposal of a racial equality clause for the new League of Nations. Despite its anger about the rebuff, the Japanese Empire emerged from the war bigger and richer than ever.

AF

JUTLAND

The Battle of Jutland (or Skagerrak, as it was known to the
Germans) took place off the Danish coast on 31 May and 1 June
1916; it was the only large-scale clash between the warships of
Britain and Germany. Although it proved a confused affair, and
although Germany claimed victory, its deeper impact was to force
Germany to revert to its **U-boats** rather than risk its High Seas
Fleet again against the British Grand Fleet. It had been German
Admiral Scheer's hope to lure out Admiral Beatty's battlecruisers
by attacking merchant shipping off Norway, and then draw
Beatty's ships onto the guns of the main High Seas Fleet. If
successful, the action would reduce the British superiority in
numbers, and Germany would have a chance to break Britain's
naval blockade. With some foreknowledge of German intentions,
the Grand Fleet under Admiral Jellicoe and Beatty's Battlecruiser
Force set sail to engage the enemy, aiming to turn the tables.
Beatty's battlecruisers (plus the 5th Battle Squadron) pursued the
German fleet commanded by Admiral Hipper, but in doing so lost
HMS *Indefatigable* and HMS *Queen Mary*. Faced with the arrival
of the main High Seas Fleet, Beatty turned away, pursued by
Scheer – who then found himself sailing directly into the line
of fire of Jellicoe's more powerful ships. In the following action
another British battlecruiser, HMS *Invincible,* was sunk, before the
Germans turned for home. Hampered by miscommunications and
the encroaching darkness, Jellicoe could not properly locate the
enemy, and while both sides lost destroyers in confused skirmishes
through the night, the High Seas Fleet crept circuitously back to
port. British losses were higher, in terms of ships and lives; but the
Royal Navy put to sea the next day, displaying a resilience that
the German fleet could not match. With rare exceptions, the
High Seas Fleet languished in port for the next two years.

IP

KAISER *to* KNITTING

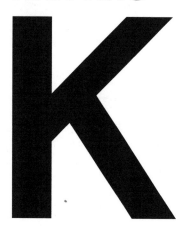

KAISER

Germany's Kaiser Wilhelm II and Britain's King George V shared at least one thing: a grandmother. As Queen Victoria's eldest grandson, 'Kaiser Bill' (1859–1941) – as he was known in Britain – came to the throne on the death of his father, Emperor Frederick, in 1888. Right from the start, the 'fabulous monster' Wilhelm (as one inter-war biographer described him) displayed a strange combination of over-confident flamboyance with depression and nervous timidity. One reflection of this was an inferiority complex as regards Britain, which motivated an obsessive competitiveness, not least to launch a large navy. Wilhelm was much given to making dramatic, boastful speeches, and his foreign visits often caused embarrassment to his hosts, despite what were described as his 'social gifts, his vivacious conversation, his prodigious versatility and energy'. During the crisis that followed the **assassination** of Archduke Franz Ferdinand, Churchill described Wilhelm's actions as being like those of a 'careless tourist who had flung down a cigarette in a powder magazine [...] a very ordinary, a vain, but on the whole well-meaning man, hoping to pass himself [off] as Frederick the Great'. With the outbreak of war, the Kaiser became the arch-demon of Allied, and especially British, **propaganda**. Every German 'atrocity' from the execution of Edith **Cavell** to the sinking of the *Lusitania* was laid personally at his door. The reality was very different. Wilhelm had little say in the principal direction of the war. When he did play a role, as with the air raids on Britain, his voice was usually one of moderation. By 1916 he had been almost completely overshadowed in executive authority by **Hindenburg** and **Ludendorff** and was reduced to making troop inspections and handing out medals. Political pressures at home, and the demands of the Allies before they would agree an armistice, forced his abdication on 9 November 1918:

he immediately went into exile in Holland, where he surprised his Dutch host by asking for 'a nice cup of English tea'. The **Versailles** Treaty called for him to be put on trial, but this never happened, and he lived out his retirement long enough to witness, and welcome, German military success in 1940.

TC

KITCHENER

In August 1914, the 64-year-old Field Marshal Lord (Horatio Herbert) Kitchener could have plausibly looked forward to resting on his imperial laurels as a colonial soldier and administrator – 'Kitchener of Khartoum', famous across the British Empire. He was about to return to his post as British overlord of Egypt when war broke out and **Asquith** offered him the post of Secretary of State for War. Kitchener reluctantly accepted, saying 'May God preserve me from politicians.' His appointment was greeted with universal acclaim. It was said that to him 'alone must be attributed the impetus which, by May 1915, had enrolled 1,700,000 men in Britain's voluntary armies'. Indeed, within days of taking office he made his first appeal for volunteers, rightly telling his colleagues that sea-power alone could not win the war, and that the country must be prepared to raise and supply armies of millions. And of course he became his own poster boy, his image used extensively for **recruitment**, its sternly pointing finger and beady eye firmly fixed on '*You*'. When he died at sea, after his ship hit a mine after leaving Scapa Flow for Russia (5 June 1916), one diarist considered it 'the worst news we have had since the war began'. But while few doubted his military skills and expertise, he was intolerant of any criticism and had an inherent inability to delegate. He was also, on his own admission, ignorant of home conditions: 'I don't know Europe; I don't know England,

and I don't know the British Army.' Kitchener was seen by some as 'the greatest Englishman of the day', but his colleagues were less sure. **Lloyd George** likened him to a lighthouse radiating 'momentary gleams of revealing light' before relapsing into complete darkness.

TC

KNITTING

All kinds of knitwear were sent in quantity to the men at the front. **Women** sent articles directly to their loved ones, but they also knitted (from around the world) for organisations such as Queen Mary's Needlework Guild, which in turn sent on the socks (718,388 pairs), balaclava helmets, mittens and many other articles it received. The beneficiaries included not only men on active service, but also their families, the wounded, refugees, prisoners of war (**POWs**) and even civilians who had lost their jobs as a result of the war. Surviving letters of thanks reveal how gratefully received these comforts often were. However, it was not always a chorus of approval. One officer in 1914 complained in a letter that 'bales' of well-intended knitwear were jamming up the postal system, and took a dim view of the 'heel-less sock'. Stockings without heels figured largely among the knitted garments needed in hospitals. They were especially wide to allow room for splints and bandages, and pattern booklets for such hospital garments were readily available, including items ranging from bath gloves to eye bandages.

MP

LAWRENCE *to*
LUSITANIA

LAWRENCE

Few names from the war years still resonate as strongly, or as paradoxically, as that of T E Lawrence (1888–1935). As 'Lawrence of Arabia', he made the conjunction of archaeology, adventure and the desert fascinating long before the era of Indiana Jones. Born Thomas Edward Lawrence, the Oxford-educated archaeologist, with officer training, was taken on by the British Army to produce maps and interrogate prisoners in the Middle East during the first two years of the war. Crucially, he became an expert on Arab nationalist movements in the Turkish provinces, from Syria south into the Hejaz, the western region of modern Saudi Arabia. By October 1916 Lawrence was charged with liaising with Prince Feisal of the Hejaz in the cause of fostering an Arab Revolt. Part middle-man between the British and Feisal, and part active guerrilla leader, his loyalties were often torn. His contribution witnessed high points (capture of the port of Aqaba, routing the Turks at Tafilah and earning the DSO, and leading the Arab Army into liberated Damascus) and low points (getting captured and – he asserted – sexually assaulted at Deraa; his disillusionment as to whether Britain and France would ever permit an independent Arab state). Undeniably, his guerrilla activity tied down huge Turkish forces across a wide area, making the British campaign through **Palestine** and into Syria easier. His romanticised post-war image stemmed first from the sensationalised reporting and film of the Arab Revolt by American journalist Lowell Thomas; and Lawrence kept his profile high with his autobiography *Seven Pillars of Wisdom* (1922). By contrast, he later sought anonymity, joining the RAF and Royal Tank Corps under assumed names. In 1935, this complex individual was fatally injured in a motorbike crash, leaving a legend that was only increased by David Lean's epic film *Lawrence of Arabia* in 1962.

RR

LETTERS

During the war, letters provided the vital link between servicemen and their families during long periods of separation. The quantity of them reflected a population that was more literate than it had ever been: in 1914 a rural British town could expect up to 12 postal deliveries a day. Serving the needs of the British Empire, the Post Office was the largest single employer of labour in the world. The British Army knew that the efficient passage of letters and parcels was vital to keeping up morale, and since the 1880s the Army Post Office Corps (part of the Royal Engineers) had administered military mail. The personnel and bodies to handle military mail mushroomed in 1914–1918, given the mammoth effort now required: in 1917 alone, over 19,000 mailbags crossed the Channel *each day*, containing letters and parcels for British troops on the **Western Front**. At the simplest level, the Army had pro-forma letters, where men could just fill in the blanks or chose from a selection of pre-printed phrases. While serving a basic need, to assure family and friends they were still alive, such forms also satisfied the military need to control the flow of information. Censorship dictated what servicemen were permitted to say in their more personal letters. However, men often found ingenious ways around it, and the surviving letters (more than 60,000 of them in IWM alone) offer powerful and highly personal insights into what it was like to live and fight through the war. They demonstrate, too, just how important the unwavering support of loved ones at home was to morale. Of course, the item of mail least welcomed was the War Office telegram, which was the most usual method of informing families of a relative's death. As one father commented in July 1916, knowing his son was fighting on the **Somme**, 'we are dreading the telegram that so many have received lately'.

EP

LICE

Body lice were an unpleasant but pervasive problem in the
trenches. The men tended to live and sleep in close proximity,
often without adequate washing facilities or sufficient spare
clothing. This created an environment ideal for lice to thrive,
laying eggs on the inside surface of clothing, which would hatch
after a week or two, whereupon the young lice could immediately
start feeding – on their host's blood. The bites could be extremely
irritating, especially if the lice were crushed and their juices
entered the wound. Worse, though, was the fact that lice could
transmit disease through their faeces – notably typhus and the
aches, lesions and sores of 'trench fever' and 'relapsing fever'.
Given that a female body louse reaches maturity in around a week
and can lay up to 300 eggs in the remaining 3–5 weeks of its life,
controlling lice was naturally difficult on the front line. Where
possible, British troops were bathed, using soap made with
paraffin or cresol, and their underclothes and service dress
uniform were placed in a disinfestor and treated with steam or
hot air at a temperature of around 80°C, in order to kill any lice
or eggs present. Both mobile and stationary disinfestors were
employed – at hospitals, bathing establishments, special
disinfesting stations, laundries, rest camps and leave billets.

MA

LIONS LED BY DONKEYS

This expression, its origins ambiguous, came to prominence with
the publication of historian (and later Conservative minister and
diarist) Alan Clark's *The Donkeys* in 1961. The phrase summed
up a view that became deeply embedded in the later twentieth-
century British psyche – of the war as a senseless bloodbath: a
stark battle of attrition, fought by courageous and heroic men
who were led by unimaginative and incompetent generals. With

a stress on the appalling conditions faced by the front-line soldier, it is a view that has informed not only the teaching of the war, but also a range of literature and journalism and stage/TV interpretations too, such as the satirical *Oh! What a Lovely War* and *Blackadder Goes Forth*. The commanders of the war, notably **Haig**, were roundly blamed for the costly failures of 1915–1917 – but given little credit for the gradual improvement and successes of 1917–1918 and the **Hundred Days Offensive** that led to final victory. Recently, revisionist historians have emphasised different qualities – a deeper understanding of the difficulties generals faced as they struggled with a war unprecedented in scale and kind; an assertion that the war, though costly, was certainly not futile; and a more nuanced view of individual successes and failures. In these ways, the 'myth' of lions led by donkeys is slowly being eroded.

SR

LLOYD GEORGE

David Lloyd George (1863–1945) was dubbed 'The Man Who Won the War', though **Churchill** preferred to call him 'the greatest Welshman which that unconquerable race has produced since the age of the Tudors' – despite his being born in Manchester. As Chancellor of the Exchequer in **Asquith**'s pre-war Liberal government he had been a radical reformer and an admirer of Germany's social welfare system. During the July 1914 crisis following the **assassination** of Archduke Franz Ferdinand, Lloyd George wanted Britain to stay neutral, but Germany's invasion of **Belgium** forced him to change his mind. With his usual ferocious and innovative energy he threw himself into the war effort, first as Chancellor, from May 1915 as Minister of Munitions, then as Secretary of State for War after **Kitchener**'s death, and finally from December 1916 as prime minister after toppling a weary Asquith. John Grigg, Lloyd George's finest biographer, has argued convincingly that when he became prime minister he was faced with a situation as black as that subsequently faced by Churchill in May 1940. And like Churchill, Lloyd George had his detractors as well as admirers. Even Lord Beaverbrook, a sympathetic friend, noted his slipperiness, writing that for Lloyd George 'no policy was permanent no pledge final. He became like a trick rider at the circus.' To many he remained 'the bounder from Wales'. Today, his great achievements during the war have tended to be overshadowed by the conflict between him and Sir Douglas **Haig**, whom he attacked mercilessly in his war memoirs, published ten years after Haig's death. But, as historian R J Q Adams observed, 'with all the power and genius which had once made him the premier social reformer of his day, Lloyd George became what democracies require from time to time: the man of peace who went to war'. And it is difficult to see how victory would have been achieved without him.

TC

LOGISTICS

'Logistics' is the collective term for the supply, movement and maintenance of armed forces – the provision of everything they depend on. The war was unprecedented in its global extent, in the size and complexity of the forces mobilised, and in the scale of operations. Consequently all belligerent states had to expand hugely their capability to support their forces with food and all the weapons, ammunition and other equipment and support needed. Thousands of miles of new railways were constructed, tens of thousands of vehicles were built or (as with London buses) requisitioned, new factories were established or existing ones expanded or 'repurposed', skills were adapted to the manufacture of war-related materials, and a complex network of depots, hospitals, ports and a myriad of other facilities was developed to support front-line operations and link them with the **home front**. Different theatres had different needs: in parts of the Middle East, infrastructure had to be created from scratch; in East **Africa**, thousands of porters struggled, and died, to carry supplies. Shortcomings in German logistics was a major factor in the ultimate failure of both the initial offensives of 1914 and those of spring 1918; initial success could not be supported long enough, giving the Allies a chance to regroup and fight back. By contrast, the ability of the Allies to push forward relentlessly from August 1918, as they began the **Hundred Days Offensive**, was a key factor in ultimate victory.

MW

LOOS *see* GAS; HAIG

LUDENDORFF

The shadow of Erich Ludendorff (1867–1937) looms large over Germany's war. Born in 1867, he became a professional soldier who, as a major on Germany's General Staff, worked on the pre-war revision of the **Schlieffen Plan**. He first came to prominence with the capture of Liège, in **Belgium**, in August 1914, but was soon transferred to the **Eastern Front**, there becoming chief-of-staff to **Hindenburg** in command of the Eighth Army. The two men, together with their brilliant staff officer Max Hoffmann, stemmed the Russian invasion of East Prussia, inflicting the costly defeats at **Tannenberg** and the Masurian Lakes. In August 1916, Ludendorff became Chief Quartermaster-General and, still in partnership with Hindenburg, virtual dictator of Germany. As such, Ludendorff was chiefly responsible for the unrestricted submarine warfare campaign, the dispatch of Lenin in a sealed train to destabilise

Russia, and the subsequent harsh terms of the Brest-Litovsk Treaty imposed on the new Bolshevik regime. Ludendorff planned and launched the last major German offensives on the **Western Front**, from 21 March 1918: his effort to defeat Britain and France before US aid became decisive. The failure of these offensives brought him to nervous collapse, and as those around him accepted the necessity of an immediate armistice, he became something of a liability; he resigned and fled to Sweden, disguised with false whiskers and dark glasses. It was not quite the end of the Ludendorff story, though. He returned to Germany in the Weimar years, fell in with Hitler and took part in his 1923 Beer Hall Putsch, and even stood as Nazi candidate against his old chief, Hindenburg, in the 1925 presidential election. But Ludendorff later broke with Hitler, and when Hindenburg appointed the Nazi leader chancellor, Ludendorff told him: 'Future generations will damn you in your grave for what you have done.'

TC

LUSITANIA

The British passenger liner *Lusitania* is a name that resonates a century after the war. When she was torpedoed by a German **U-boat** on 7 May 1915, the ship became a *cause célèbre*, cited as yet more proof of German vileness and a contributing factor in swaying American opinion away from neutrality. RMS *Lusitania* was *en route* from New York to Liverpool when she was attacked by the submarine *U-20* off the south coast of Ireland. She sank in just 20 minutes, and 1,201 men, women and children lost their lives. That number included 128 Americans and 80 per cent of all children on board. On 22 April, the German Embassy in Washington had issued a general warning that ships bound for Britain were liable to be sunk on sight, as part of its policy of unrestricted submarine warfare to blockade Britain. And *Lusitania* had been registered with the British Admiralty as an 'Armed Auxiliary Cruiser'; on her final voyage she was carrying a small cargo of munitions. But the British Admiralty failed to warn *Lusitania* that U-boats were operating in the area, despite two ships being attacked the previous day. The sinking was seen in Britain and America as little short of murder, provoking a wave of bitter anti-German **propaganda**. Relations between Germany and the **United States** deteriorated and, though not sufficient cause – yet – to bring America into the war, the memory of *Lusitania* was long.

AR

MACHINE GUN *to* MUNITIONETTES

MACHINE GUN

Machine guns existed before 1914, and the British used them in their colonial wars. But the technology came into its own during the First World War, and on the battlefield the machine gun became the second biggest killer of men, after **artillery**. The machine gun remains an enduring symbol of the conflict and of its industrialised killing. The first guns of the war, such as the British Vickers, adapted from the Maxim, were heavy machine guns (HMGs). They needed a team of men to operate and move them, so were used primarily in defence, and they fired in bursts to rake an area or a line. They were best placed so that they could provide overlapping fields of fire, and machine-gun positions became integrated into trench design. The Germans led the way in this respect, positioning guns in their concrete bunkers. Indeed, machine guns played a significant role in the imbalance of strength between attacking and defending forces, which made defensive positions so hard to break in trench warfare. Fired at knee-height at attacking infantry over open ground, the guns could be devastating. As the war progressed, units carried larger complements of machine guns, and the machine gun's role became more versatile – mounted on **aeroplanes** and in **tanks**. And light machine guns (LMGs) appeared, of greater use to forces on the attack because they were more portable and operable by one person: the Lewis Gun was an excellent example. Eventually some armies were using sub-machine guns (SMGs) as well, personal weapons as portable as a rifle. The British developed new tactics, too, of using machine guns as quasi-artillery – firing at enemy positions over the heads of their advancing troops.

LDM

MAPS

In an era long before GPS, the role of maps and mapping was crucial to military conduct, from **logistics** to battle-planning. Millions of military maps, as well as commercial maps about the war for press, propaganda and educational use, were produced between 1914 and 1918. As the war's weapons became more advanced so did the mapping techniques. The development of aerial **photography** placed a premium on controlling the skies, because maps from those photographs could help determine **artillery** targets and infantry tactics. Specialist cartographers were sent to the front lines to help develop new techniques. Among their tasks was constant surveying in order to map every detail of relevant areas and plot the trenches, guns and batteries of both sides. Lawrence Bragg, who did so much to advance the technique of sound-ranging to locate enemy guns, worked for the much expanded Maps GHQ on the Western Front; and T E **Lawrence** was mapping the Middle East before he found fame in other ways. The diverse maps of the war tell their own fascinating stories and sub-stories of the conflict: the path of an air raid, the density of graves in a small corner of the Somme, the enemy's order of battle, the snaking tendrils of trenchlines or a web of rail lines, or the loud pictorial maps for **propaganda** that depicted the enemy as national stereotypes or even animals.

BP

MARNE

Two of the most decisive battles of the war were fought along the River Marne, a 325-mile-long tributary of the Seine. The first took place at the beginning of September 1914. With Paris under direct threat from the invading Germans, French Commander-in-Chief Joffre ordered an Allied counter-attack. In a dramatic move, French troops were even rushed to the front in Parisian taxi cabs. A series of interrelated actions proceeded, as the French and British fought the Germans (under their generals Kluck and Bülow), whose troops could see the Eiffel Tower in the distance. The battle climaxed on 9 September, and the Germans were ordered to fall back. This 'Miracle of the Marne', as it was soon to be known, not only saved Paris, but also dashed the German strategy for a speedy victory over **France** as embodied in its **Schlieffen Plan**. The war of attrition, in which trench faced trench, was about to begin. The Second Battle of the Marne was fought almost exactly four years later, between 15 July and 7 August 1918. In what was to prove **Ludendorff**'s last offensive in the West, his troops attempted a two-pronged attack across the Marne and advanced as far as Château-Thierry. But the Allies were ready, and the French, British and Americans halted the attack, before Franco-American forces converged in a successful counter-offensive on 18 July. The Germans, as in 1914, were driven back, and soon the Allied advance of the **Hundred Days Offensive** would prove unstoppable.

TC

MASCOTS

Numerous mascots were taken on by military forces during the war, providing relief, inspiration and something around which to unite. Intriguing stories are attached to many of them. Jimmy 'the Sergeant', a donkey, was found during the Somme: soldiers in the Cameronian Scottish Rifles raised him on tins of condensed milk and taught him to raise his hoof, in a salute, on command. He was wounded three times but survived the war. And he was not the only donkey to do duty as a mascot. Unsurprisingly, cats and dogs were common mascots both on land and on ships, but goats were popular too. More exotically, there were also a number of bears. One adorned the battleship HMS *Royal Oak* , and a

Canadian lieutenant brought a bear cub named 'Winnie' over to France. Winnie then became a regimental mascot in England; when Christopher Milne later saw her at London Zoo, the inspiration behind a fictional bear was born. Other animal mascots included lemurs, parrots, foxes, pigs and even hedgehogs. But mascots did not necessarily need to be *live* animals; the cock that Commander Max Horton of the British submarine *M.1* owned was made of silver. Nor were mascots the exclusive domain of soldiers and sailors. Nurses at the Royal Hospital in Granton adopted a stuffed toy cat as their mascot.

SJ

MATA HARI

The story of Mata Hari (1876–1917), with its mixture of espionage, sex, money and war, was made to intrigue. This Dutch exotic dancer and mistress of important men was executed by the French in 1917, after being tried as a German spy. She was blamed for the deaths of many Allied soldiers. Yet murk and mystery still surround her. Born Margaretha Zelle, she spoke several languages and travelled frequently, helped by her status as a neutral. In 1903 she left Holland and her marriage to pursue a dancing career in Paris, equipped with shimmering veils and a metallic bra. Sexual allure and money became inextricable, as her lifestyle depended to a large extent on the favours of lovers. When war came she had been performing for several months in Berlin and enjoying the attentions of German officers, too. She made her way back to France, via Holland and England, but not before accepting money to spy for the Germans (whether she *did* spy for them is not known) and arousing the suspicions of the British, who interrogated her. Back in Paris, she was desperately in love with a Russian officer and needed French permission to visit him, near the war zone; and she was deeply in debt. To solve both problems she agreed with the French head of counter-intelligence, Georges Ladoux, to use her freedom of movement and seduction skills to spy for France in return for money. He later claimed this was his ruse to trap her, for she was already under surveillance. Her arrest came on 13 February 1917. At her trial, her dealings with a German officer in Spain were alleged to be, not pro-French espionage as she claimed, but working for the enemy. She was found guilty and thrown into a dismal prison cell, before being shot in a muddy field on 17 February. Was she a spy who ensured the deaths of thousands of soldiers? Or was she simply a larger-than-life personality who craved love, attention and money? Her guilt is still debated.

SJ

MEDICINE

Military medicine during the First World War was decidedly *military*, with strict rules, systems and hierarchies. From the moment soldiers were wounded they became part of a huge medical-administrative machine. The priority was to heal soldiers as quickly as possible so that they could return to the front, and a labelling system ('triage') was developed to do this as efficiently as possible: its legacy lives on today in hospitals, although the priority now is to treat those with the greatest need first. Some men could be treated near the front, at casualty clearing stations. The more seriously ill and wounded were ferried further afield, and for British and Imperial troops this could mean back to Britain, to be distributed among hospitals and facilities. For hospitalised patients, life was about more than just healing the physical wounds of war. Some of them even compiled humorous magazines making fun of hospital life, an activity encouraged by staff, and sports and other distracting events were organised. The huge numbers of sick and wounded generated by war provided medical professionals with a unique challenge and opportunity to try new techniques and technologies. And so the period 1914–1918 saw developments in blood transfusions, **X-rays**, surgery, facial reconstruction and **prosthetics**, and the treatment of infections. Other developments had an impact too: the introduction of steel helmets ironically generated more head wounds for the doctors to deal with, because men were surviving injuries when previously they would have been killed. And new bodies of volunteer **nurses** sprang up. But advances were not across the board, and the rigours of war meant that medical training and the quality of treatment could be patchy. The huge numbers of casualties and rapid spread of **disease** forced surgeons to work quickly and in trying conditions, making decisions that could often sit uneasily with their professional ethics. It was sometimes easier, quicker and more practical to amputate a limb (and move on to the next patient) than to try and save it.

EH & AL

MESOPOTAMIA

The Turkish province of Mesopotamia (modern Iraq) was a theatre of the war that witnessed mixed fortunes for the British Imperial forces, which had to combat not only enemy troops, but also heat, **disease** and an almost complete absence of infrastructure. Immediately on **Turkey**'s entry into the war, Indian Expeditionary Force 'D' landed near Basra, in November 1914, to secure the nearby oilfields that were vital for fuelling the Royal Navy's most modern warships. Then forces under General Sir John Nixon, spurred on by the ambitious British government of India, began advancing along the River Tigris, getting within 20 miles of Baghdad. Leading the troops, Major General Sir Charles Townshend relied more on bluff and the incompetence of Turkish forces than on sound strategy and tactics, and he was forced to retreat after the Battle of Ctesiphon (22–25 November 1915) before suffering a disastrous siege in Kut-al-Amara. Increasingly desperate attempts by relief forces to save Townshend's men in early January 1916 came up against the strongly entrenched Turkish positions, along the Tigris.

On 29 April 1916, Townshend bowed to the inevitable and surrendered Kut. His men paid a heavy price, many subsequently dying on forced marches as **POWs**. The failure stiffened British resolve, however, and – now under the political direction of London rather than Delhi – men and material poured into Mesopotamia for a new offensive. It began on 13 December 1916, under Lieutenant General Sir Stanley Maude, and this time resulted in the capture of Baghdad in March 1917, before forces pushed on northwards. Final hostilities, at the Battle of Sharqat, ended when Turkey took itself out of the war by agreeing the armistice at Moudros (30 October 1918) – though the temptation for the Imperial forces to advance a few miles further and occupy Mosul proved irresistible.

AW

MESSINES

Messines Ridge, south-east of **Ypres**, was the scene of a successful British attack by General Herbert Plumer's Second Army in 1917. Plumer had been planning to take this natural strongpoint since mid-1916. He envisaged a limited operation by using the full panoply of **artillery, tanks** and **gas** to minimise British casualties. The centrepiece was to be the explosion of 20 huge mines planted under the German lines. Starting in January 1917, no less than 8,000 metres of tunnel were dug, despite German counter-mining and the discovery of one mine, which was blown up. The remaining 19 were filled with 600 tons of explosive. After a preliminary bombardment, the mines were detonated at 3.10am on the morning of 7 June 1917. So powerful was the blast, it was said that **Lloyd George** heard it at 10 Downing Street. An estimated 10,000 German soldiers died, and 9 advancing British infantry divisions took all their first objectives in under 3 hours. The Germans unsuccessfully counter-attacked the next day, and a week later the entire Messines salient was in British hands. It was a welcome boost to Allied morale; it was also the first battle on the **Western Front** since 1914 in which the attacking forces lost fewer men (17,000) than the defenders (25,000). Lloyd George called Messines 'a clean victory, in the sense that it was a victory without any qualification or reserve'.

TC

MONS

In a strangely neat twist of fate, the Belgian town of Mons was where the British first began fighting on the **Western Front**, and it was where some of them ended up again at the time of the **Armistice**; at Mons the first and last British servicemen killed on the front fell, just yards from each other. Events began when, on 22 August 1914, the Germans threw the French back from Namur, and a breach appeared in the Allied line, leaving Field Marshal Sir John French's **BEF** isolated at Mons. Four German corps attacked Sir John's men at 9am the next day, one of mist and drizzle, but it was claimed that 'the excellence of British rifle and artillery fire stemmed a frontal attack'. Rumours abounded of a mystical 'Angel of Mons' emerging from the mist to protect the Tommies. A machine-gun officer in the Scottish Borderers wrote: 'This was our first experience of killing people; it was rather horrible, but satisfactory.' On the German side, Walther Bloem, an army captain, described how: 'The enemy […] had artfully enticed us to close range […] A hellish fire broke loose. Wherever I looked, to the right or left, nothing but dead, and blood-streaming, sobbing, writhing wounded.' Despite this initial British success, a German encircling movement compelled Sir John to order a retreat, which began on 24 August 'amid desperate fighting all along the 20–25 mile front'. British casualties at Mons amounted to 1,600, and despite the retreat Mons was to take its place alongside Blenheim and Waterloo in British military lore. On 11 November 1918, before the guns fell silent, the 2nd Battalion of the Royal Irish Regiment found themselves battling the Germans once again at Mons; they had been there on 23 August 1914.

TC

MUD

Men and animals wading in mud, living in mud, amid landscapes once carpeted with trees and meadows but now churned by **artillery** into featureless mud – these have become imprinted on our consciousness as the defining environment of the war. In one sense it was undeniably true. The **trenches** on the **Western Front** meant that men lived semi-subterranean lives, while elsewhere, as at **Gallipoli**, the necessity to 'dig in' combined with bad weather meant an often muddy existence too. And while German forces, consolidating their occupied territory, built concrete living quarters, Allied trenches were usually not as well protected from the elements. But different regions produced different terrain and different experiences. Flanders, with its high water table and destroyed drainage ditches, did produce powerful scenes of sodden misery, reaching their apogee during the battle over **Passchendaele**. The chalk-filled landscape of the Somme, however, was a different matter – as of course were the forests of the Argonne, the deserts of the Sinai, Arabia and

Mesopotamia, the plains of Poland and the Ukraine, the mountains of the Italian–Austrian border, or the bush, scrub and jungle of East Africa.

EA

MUNITIONS

All the main contenders in the war came to realise that the fight for victory was to a large extent a fight to manufacture more bullets and ammunition than the enemy. The British realised this painfully. On 10 March 1915, they launched an offensive on the Western Front at Neuve Chapelle. Despite initial success, the attack was called off after only three days, one of the main reasons given (and publicised in the press) being that British artillery lacked sufficient shells. The ensuing 'Shell Scandal', in which **Kitchener** and his War Office were blamed for the shortages, helped push **Asquith**'s Liberal government into a coalition with the Conservatives on 25 May, and now **Lloyd George** left the Treasury to take charge of a new Ministry of Munitions. With the powers granted to him by the Munitions of War Act, he took greater control over labour, capital, raw materials and machinery than any Cabinet minister until that time. To cut through red tape, talented outsiders – styled by the press as 'Men of Push and Go' – joined the Ministry, Lloyd George telling an audience: 'When the house is on fire, questions of procedure and precedence, of etiquette and time and division of labour must disappear.' Under his dynamic leadership munitions production soared. In the first half year he was in office, shell production more than doubled to 5.38 million, and 6 months later it was up to nearly 14 million. To increase production, women – the **munitionettes** – were recruited in ever larger numbers.

TC

MUNITIONETTES

Once Britain's Ministry of **Munitions** was established in the summer of 1915, and the munitions-related factories mushroomed, ever greater numbers of **women** flocked to meet the need for labour. This was especially so after 1916, when the introduction of conscription diverted men to the armed forces. The female munitions workers were nicknamed 'munitionettes', echoing 'suffragettes'. Many of them appreciated the opportunity to do their bit for the war effort and directly support their men at the front. It could also be relatively well-paid work (though women always earned less than the men) and offer welcome social and welfare benefits; and it frequently gave an independence that was new to many women. At the same time, the work itself had dangers, including the risk of poisoning. Exposure to the high explosive 'trinitrotoluene' – TNT – discoloured both skin and hair, so that, in the words of one worker, 'It was all bright ginger, all our front hair, and our faces were bright yellow. They used to call us "canaries".' While the Battle of the **Somme** was being fought in 1916, concern about the high casualty rates from TNT poisoning in the factories (52 deaths that year) resulted in new cleanliness and ventilation regulations. These and other measures saw death rates from poisoning fall to 44 in 1917 and 10 in 1918. But accidents with machinery and occasional deadly factory explosions (more than 130 workers killed in one 1918 incident at Chilwell, Nottinghamshire) added to the potential dangers. For the vast majority of women who survived the perils, their wartime experience was an important, even transforming, experience. After the war, women increasingly shunned domestic service, their horizons having been broadened (and their wage packets increased) by their war work.

SP

NO MAN'S LAND *to* NURSES

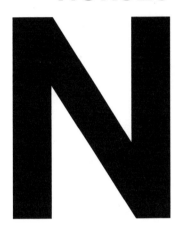

NEUVE CHAPELLE *see* MUNITIONS

NEW ZEALAND *see* ANZAC

NO MAN'S LAND

Between the lines of forward **trenches** and **barbed wire** in the
First World War lay that dangerous space called 'no man's land'
separating the combatants. It could be just a few hundred yards
wide, both sides easily visible to one another should they –
foolishly – raise their heads above the parapet. The physical
qualities of no man's land varied, depending on the theatre of war,
the geology and topography, the weather and time of year, and
the intensity of any fighting. In **Gallipoli** it was the dry, dusty
and rocky ground typical of the peninsula in summer, while on
the **Western Front** it could be a grassy field, a desolate wood or a
few scattered tree stumps, some derelict buildings or a pummelled
morass of shell holes. At least the ruins and shell holes provided
soldiers with a small amount of shelter from bullets – though
when unfortunate Newfoundlanders sought shelter behind a tree
during the **Somme** campaign, they merely became a congregated
target for German **machine guns**. Open fields, as on the Somme,
could also make slow-moving waves of attackers sitting ducks.
When heavy rainfall filled shell holes, men could drown in them
or – especially if already wounded – become infected in the dirty
water. Many shell holes still remain visible in the landscape. If by
day no man's land was avoided, except during an offensive, by
night it was a relative hive of activity. Then, soldiers entered it,
under cover of darkness, for raiding parties, to reconnoitre the
enemy, to fix broken wire or implant new wire, sometimes to
launch small-scale attacks, and often to reach the remaining
wounded. Despite best efforts, after a large offensive the maimed
and dying could linger for days out there without treatment,

risking sniper fire, bombardment, infection and starvation. But there were also instances of sudden camaraderie between enemies too, finding themselves thrown together in the inhospitable space of no man's land.

SJ

NURSES

With the outbreak of war, the British Army needed nurses as never before. Reforms after the Crimean War, inspired by Florence Nightingale, had led to the establishment of a professional Army nursing service, and in their grey and scarlet uniforms the Queen Alexandra's Imperial Military Nursing Service numbered 290 in 1914. Their numbers now multiplied, with a Reserve that grew to nearly 8,000 by November 1918. The Territorial Force Nursing Service was initially deployed at home, while military and naval nurses were supported by Voluntary Aid Detachments (VADs) of the British Red Cross Society or Order of St John. They served in hospitals, casualty clearing stations and on hospital ships, barges and trains, and they comprised many roles apart from nursing. Agatha Christie served as a dispenser of drugs, and learned much that would be handy for her later career writing detective fiction; and the autobiographer Vera Brittain was one of the volunteers who took first-aid courses and gained practical experience on the wards. Often young and attractive, the women of the VADs earned their acronym an alternative translation: 'Very Adorable Darlings'. Not all women who wanted to were able to serve with British organisations. After Dr Elsie Inglis had been turned down by the War Office, the French authorities eagerly accepted her Scottish Women's Hospitals – staffed entirely by women. Some women even acted independently, celebrated examples being the keen motorcyclists Elsie Knocker (later Baroness T'Serclaes) and Mairi Chisholm, who set up their own first aid post just behind the front line in the village of Pervyse, in Belgium. They were each awarded the Military Medal for their work there, before a gas attack forced their return to Britain in 1918, whereupon they undertook further service in the Women's Royal Air Force. The war's most famous nurse, though, was Edith **Cavell**, whose execution gave the Allies a martyr and a **propaganda** triumph.

SP

OH! WHAT A LOVELY WAR
to OLD BILL

OH! WHAT A LOVELY WAR

Oh! What a Lovely War was a 1963 'musical entertainment' about the First World War, developed and performed by Joan Littlewood's pioneering Theatre Workshop ensemble. It began at their humble Theatre Royal Stratford East, in London, before transferring to the West End in 1964, and then crossing the ocean to become a Tony-nominated Broadway show. It was later developed (1969) into a star-studded British film directed by Richard Attenborough. Although it was a freewheeling mixture of theatrical styles, for its content it drew on speeches, statements and soldiers' (often irreverent) **songs** from the war, such as the ditty 'Hanging on the Old Barbed Wire': 'If you want to find the old battalion, I know where they are [...] they're hanging on the old barbed wire'. The show delivered an anti-war message very much in tune with its era's **'lions led by donkeys'** sense of history, contrasting the pomposity and incompetence of politicians and generals with the experiences of the ordinary **Tommy**. According to one of the original actors, Victor Spinetti, Princess Margaret observed of the West End production: 'Well Miss Littlewood those things should have been said many years ago.' The Theatre Royal mounted a 50th-anniversary production for the centenary of the outbreak of the First World War, in 2014.

EF

OLD BILL

The cartoon figure 'Old Bill' was the archetype of the British **Tommy**, created by Captain Bruce Bairnsfather of the Royal Warwickshire Regiment, and first appearing in *Bystander* magazine in 1915. Old Bill, with his lugubrious nature and ironic humour, immediately caught the public's imagination, and Bairnsfather was later described by General Sir Ian Hamilton as 'the man who made the Empire laugh in its darkest hour'. Old

Bill was quickly merchandised, appearing on mugs, ashtrays, shaving mugs and other china and pottery items as well as mascots and dolls. In 1926, a London bus which had transported troops on the Western Front was even renamed 'Old Bill' (now part of IWM's collections, the bus is currently on display at the London Transport Museum). Old Bill featured, too, in the huge stage success *The Better 'Ole*, partly written by Bairnsfather and later filmed, where the character was played by Arthur Bouchier. A critic wrote: 'It is a tribute to the essential truthfulness of Captain Bairnsfather's conception and Mr Bouchier's acting that one comes away from *The Better 'Ole* feeling that there must be thousands of Old Bills at the front fighting for our freedom.' Bairnsfather maintained that Old Bill was a figment of his own imagination, but Tonie and Valmai Holt in their biography of Bairnsfather present a strong case for Lance Corporal Thomas Henry 'Pat' Rafferty being the model. Rafferty served in Bairnsfather's battalion, was killed on 25 April 1915 and is commemorated on the Menin Gate.

TC

PALESTINE *to* PROSTHETICS

PALESTINE

Intermittently, between 1915 and 1918, British and Imperial forces of the Egyptian Expeditionary Force (EEF) – aided on their flank by the Arab irregulars under Prince Feisal and T E **Lawrence** – fought their way from the Sinai Peninsula through Ottoman-ruled Palestine and Syria. It was, to begin with, a counter-offensive, after Turkish and German forces had attempted in January 1915 to seize the Suez Canal, Britain's strategic imperial artery and lifeline to India. A stalemate then existed east of the canal, until in late 1917 the EEF, under General Sir Edmund Allenby, began a bloody push north through Gaza until finally entering Jerusalem. (The mayor's improvised white surrender flag is now in IWM's collections.) The symbolic city surrendered on 9 December 1917, and Allenby entered on foot, to show humility and respect for its status in three world religions. It was all very different to the **Western Front**: with little infrastructure, the advance depended on constructing a water pipeline, an improvised road and a rail line. The fighting, by a highly multinational force against Turkish and some German troops, also witnessed classic cavalry manoeuvres as well as camel charges. Reinforced by Indian troops during the summer of 1918, Allenby's men launched an offensive in September; in under 40 days they advanced 350 miles. With RAF support and clever switching of cavalry from flank to flank, they effectively routed two Turkish armies at the Battle of Megiddo, took control of the region's lifeline – the Hejaz Railway – and even nearly captured the German commander-in-chief. On 1 October Damascus fell, and Arab forces made a ceremonial entry to take control of the city they viewed as their future capital. But in the **Sykes–Picot** agreement, the British and French had other ideas about shaping the Middle East.

GR

PALS

Pals battalions were a notable feature of the British **recruitment** effort during 1914–1916. At the start of the war, Britain had a decidedly small (but professional) army in comparison with the large Continental conscript armies. To boost the numbers of volunteers, men were encouraged to sign up with their friends, neighbours and workmates. From London stockbrokers to Lancashire mill workers, men throughout Britain joined up in groups linked by friendship, locality or profession, under the promise that they would serve together. After training, for many Pals their first taste of actual action was on the **Somme** in 1916. The losses there brought home the tragic dimension of the Pals exercise: while the bonds within the groups helped morale and cohesiveness, they also meant that loss and grief were concentrated in those same groups, and in their families and friends back home. Notoriously, of the 700 men of the Accrington Pals (from the Lancashire town of that name) who went into action on 1 July 1916, 585 were killed or injured within just 20 minutes. In some towns and villages, almost every street and community was affected by the loss of Pals who, having joined up and served together, now died together. The Pals approach to recruiting was to be shelved, and anyway **conscription** became the response to the manpower problem.

cc

PASSCHENDAELE

'Passchendaele' – a name redolent of the worst of the **Western Front**'s conditions – is something of a misnomer. It has been applied to the whole of the Third Battle of **Ypres** launched by the British on 31 July 1917 to take control of ridges south and west of Ypres. In fact, the battle over the village of Passchendaele was just the final, albeit ghastly, part of the campaign. Yet it remains a modern synonym for disaster and the futility of war, its memories dominated by images of **mud** and death. August was unusually wet, and in the whole month of October 1917 there were only seven days without rain. The water clogged the ground, with its already high water table, and the British Army's own preliminary bombardment made it worse. This degeneration of the terrain slowed everything, including the transport of supplies, the movement of men and the ability to fight. It is from Passchendaele that we have those evocative images of men gingerly treading along duckboards, surrounded by a quagmire of water and mud, or **horses** struggling for survival having slipped off the narrow slivers of firm ground. **Tanks** became immobile too. Garish occurrences of men drowning did happen, but these were relatively infrequent. At least the troops were regularly relieved in the line. Militarily, and despite the appalling conditions, the battle was a mixture of success and failure: ground was taken and on 7 November 1917 Canadians captured Passchendaele Ridge. After the huge sacrifices of the Third Battle of Ypres – about 396,000 casualties – the British and Imperial forces began the winter having gained well-drained land and the commanding heights. And the heavy toll on the German defenders, estimated at almost 350,000 casualties, shocked **Ludendorff**.

SJ

PEACE CONFERENCE *see* CANADA; ITALY; JAPAN; REPARATIONS; VERSAILLES

PÉTAIN

Philippe Pétain (1856–1951) had had a relatively undistinguished military career and was on the point of retiring with the rank of colonel when the war broke out. He quickly gained a reputation as one of the more successful French generals on the **Western Front**; but it was as commander of the relentless struggle to defend **Verdun** between February and April 1916 that he achieved nationwide fame. Following the failure and casualties of General Robert Nivelle's offensive in the spring of 1917, and the ensuing mutinies in the French Army, Pétain replaced Nivelle as commander-in-chief on 15 May. He immediately set about remedying the conditions that had led to the mutinies, improving the soldiers' food and leave allowances, and restricting the Army to defensive operations, telling his troops: 'We must wait for the Americans and the tanks.' However, Pétain gained the reputation of being defeatist. Although still commander-in-chief he was subordinated to **Foch**, and had only a comparatively minor role in the planning of the final successful **Hundred Days Offensive**. Nevertheless, he was created a Marshal of France two weeks after the **Armistice**, still a *bona fide* French hero. It was a bitter coda to his reputation and career that in the next war he led the collaborationist Vichy regime following France's defeat by Nazi Germany, for which he was sentenced to death in August 1945 – a verdict commuted to a prison sentence by General Charles de Gaulle, who had been a junior officer in Pétain's regiment in 1914. The old hero of Verdun died in 1951 having, in the words of one biographer, 'outlived his glory and his shame'.

TC

PHOTOGRAPHY

The First World War was the first conflict to be photographed in detail by all the participant nations. When war broke out in 1914, the skills and technology required to photograph it were mostly in place. Photography was a popular hobby practiced by millions and a thriving professional industry, involving large numbers of press and portrait photographers. Militarily, photography had clear uses for intelligence-gathering and campaign-planning. It was vital to try and find out where the enemy's strengths and weaknesses lay, where the trench networks and machine-gun emplacements were, and where troops and supplies were moving. As **aeroplane** technology developed, cameras were fitted to aircraft, resulting in thousands of aerial photographs – valuable resources to this day. Photography as a way of documenting the war and presenting it to the public was less clear-cut. Initially governments and military leaders were reluctant to permit photography in the war zone for any non-military purpose and failed to recognise its wider potential in the war effort, as a medium of mass communication. But people wanted to see, as well as read about, events, and it proved impossible to exclude cameras completely. Arrangements for official documentary and **propaganda** photography were therefore established. Although military photographers were the only professionals consistently allowed to work in the front line, men and women in uniform used personal snapshot cameras, too, to record their experiences. As the war progressed, photographers overcame the limitations and restrictions to set precedents that would be followed by photographers of subsequent conflicts.

HR

PIGEONS

Homing pigeons – over 100,000 of them used by the British alone – served in the war effort in their traditional message-carrying role, especially when the more modern (but often unreliable) means of communications were not practicable. It has been estimated that 95 per cent of pigeons reached their destinations successfully. Their homing abilities and agility made them an invaluable resource, especially when the battle was characterised by movement, as on the **Western Front** in 1914 and again in 1918. At the First Battle of the **Marne**, for example, French troops brought 72 lofts with them as they pushed the Germans back, and despite the troops' frequent change of location all 'on duty' pigeons made it back to their lofts. The lofts could be in unusual places, too – even London buses were converted to house pigeons. Occasionally individual pigeons found fame, a well-known example being 'Cher Ami', whose message-carrying exploits allowed 194 US troops to be rescued after being stranded behind enemy lines in 1918, a feat that earned the bird the Croix de Guerre.

LM

POETRY

In Britain, a century on, the popular impression of the First World War owes much to the widespread influence of the emotive poetry written by soldier-poets such as Edmund Blunden, Robert Graves, Siegfried Sassoon and, perhaps the greatest of them all, Wilfred Owen. Indeed, historians have often lamented the degree to which poetry has 'colonised' impressions of the war. Yet the first of the poets to capture the public's imagination was Rupert Brooke. His war poems, in complete contrast to Sassoon's and Owen's, epitomised a romantic and idealised view of warfare held by many in Britain in 1914: 'Now, God be thanked Who has matched us with His hour, / And caught our Youth, and wakened us from sleeping.' Brooke joined the Royal Naval Division, and in April 1915 met a tragically early death (from illness) *en route* to **Gallipoli**, so he did not experience the war's terrible attrition. Two years later, Wilfred Owen's 'Dulce et Decorum Est' was written, bringing home the bitter realities of war and challenging Brooke's patriotic idealism:

If you could hear, at every jolt, the blood
Come gargling from the froth-corrupted lungs,
[…]
My friend, you would not tell with such high zest
To children ardent for some desperate glory,
The old Lie: Dulce et decorum est
Pro patria mori.

TC

POPPIES

The poppy is *the* enduring symbol of remembrance of the First
World War, and the artificial kind is worn widely in the weeks
around 11 November each year. Its origin as a symbol lies in the
landscapes of the First World War, where poppies flourished in
the disturbed soil caused by shelling and fighting. The flower
inspired the Canadian Doctor John McCrae's popular 1915 poem
'In Flanders Fields' ('In Flanders Fields, the poppies blow /
Between the crosses, row on row'), published in *Punch* magazine.
It was a French woman, Madame Guerin, who hit on the idea of
manufacturing and selling artificial poppies for charitable
purposes, originally for French war orphans. In the United States,
Moina Michael took up the idea in 1918 and even wrote a poem
in response to McCrae's ('And now the Torch and Poppy Red /
We wear in honor of our dead'). Another adopter was Earl **Haig**'s
Fund for ex-servicemen and the families of those who had died in
the conflict. In 1922 the (Royal) British Legion founded a factory,
staffed by disabled ex-servicemen, to manufacture poppies – as it
still does today. The poppy, as with Remembrance Day itself, now
symbolises all modern wars from 1914.

HM

POSTERS

It was during the First World War that governments first fully exploited the techniques of advertising and the mass media as part of a concerted **propaganda** campaign. Britain was well placed, in that it had a well-established advertising industry, and posters now appeared on an unprecedented scale. The recruitment effort was an immediate priority. The first call to enlist came days after the outbreak of war, and within a fortnight the Parliamentary Recruiting Committee (PRC) was established under the supervision of Hedley Le Bas of the Caxton (Advertising) Agency. He delegated the devising and design of campaigns to agencies or printing houses, and by the time **conscription** was introduced in 1916 the PRC had overseen 164 poster designs, manifested in 12.5 million posters. They generally combined high moral values with sharp graphic design, and had images and slogans that emphasised patriotic duty, the devilishness of the Germans and the trampling of **Belgium** ('Remember Belgium – Enlist Today!', 'Take Up the Sword of Justice!' or 'Women of Britain Say "Go!"'). None, though, became more famous than the poster featuring **Kitchener**'s implacable face and pointing finger, an image adapted from a 1914 magazine cover. After conscription, the PRC was transformed into the Parliamentary War Savings Committee, and it now encouraged people to invest in government bonds to support the war effort ('Lend Your Savings to the Nation Today!' or 'Back Them Up – Invest in the War Loan'). The advertising agencies' approach tended to target ordinary people's sense of solidarity, community and – as with the recruitment campaign – duty. Inevitably, the posters conveyed relatively simplistic messages, and even before war's end a certain disillusionment with state-inspired propaganda set in, as the human cost of the war became more apparent.

VT

POWs

The first prisoners of war in 1914 were civilians caught in the
wrong place at war's outbreak: crews from merchant vessels,
tourists, students, business people, and those who had long-
established homes (and dual nationality) in what was now an
enemy country, were all rounded up into camps. In Germany, the
racecourse at Ruhleben, just outside Berlin, became the largest
civilian internment camp, holding over 5,000 internees. In Britain
mass internment began only in May 1915, following the
torpedoing of the *Lusitania*. Alexandra Palace in London and
Knockaloe on the Isle of Man became the largest 'enemy alien'
camps. During August 1914, the war's opening offensives
generated tens of thousands of military POWs, notably Russians
and French after the battles of **Tannenberg** and the Frontiers
respectively. While unfortunate for the captured, this was also a
major logistical challenge for the captors. During the war, about
192,000 British and Imperial servicemen became POWs. Most
(over 175,000) were taken on the **Western Front**, with the largest
number being captured during the German offensives in spring
1918. The pre-war Hague and Geneva Conventions laid the basis
of how prisoners should be treated, and officers came off
distinctly better; other ranks were obliged to work for their
captors, often in miserable conditions. Red Cross parcels provided
both moral and physical sustenance that undoubtedly saved lives.
But the treatment of Allied prisoners in **Turkey** was particularly
harsh – it has been estimated that over 70 per cent of British and
Imperial POWs (many of them Indians) died in, or on the way
to, Turkish camps, including on the notorious forced march
following the siege of Kut in 1915. It is not generally known that
there were more successful escapes from Germany in the First
World War than there were during the longer 1939–1945 conflict.
The most successful single breakout was from Holzminden on

23 July 1918. Twenty-nine officers got away from the camp through a sixty-yard tunnel, before it collapsed; while nineteen were recaptured, the other ten made it to neutral Holland.

SP

PROPAGANDA

The scale of the war committed its main nations to **total war**, demanding economic, industrial and human obligations on an unprecedented scale. Just as maintaining morale was recognised as important to an army's efficiency, so **propaganda** on the **home fronts** began to emerge as the principal instrument of control over public opinion. Governments knew they had to 'sell' their messages about why they were going to war, what they were demanding from the people, and why they were continuing the war. To persuade men to enlist, **women** to work in the factories, civilians to buy war bonds, and to undermine the enemy's cause and bolster one's own in international opinion – all fuelled an active British propaganda campaign that embraced all the media. Conservatives in Britain tended to see the war as defending the Empire, while liberals, outraged by the trampling of Belgian neutrality, saw it as a struggle for democracy. Both ideas fed the propaganda – as in **posters** showing the 'young lions' of the Empire's Dominions coming to aid the 'old lion' of the mother country, or the many explicit references to a violated **Belgium**. In 1915 the British government published the Bryce Report, which confirmed allegations of German murder, wanton destruction and rape in **Belgium** and **France**. The 'atrocity' theme became prevalent in newspapers and posters, fed by the execution of Edith **Cavell** and the sinking of the *Lusitania.* The press by and large acquiesced in printing official or uncritical reports about the front, and in February 1918 a Ministry of Information was formally established under press magnate Lord Beaverbrook.

Of course, as the war ground on the initial stridency of propaganda had to make way for something more sophisticated. Nevertheless, the war left an uncomfortable legacy. The public became mistrustful of propaganda, realising that conditions at the front had been deliberately obscured behind patriotic slogans and that accounts of enemy atrocities had been exaggerated. By contrast, Adolf Hitler later put Germany's defeat in part down to a disintegration of German morale led by a skilful British propaganda campaign.

VT

PROSTHETICS

Much innovation was spurred by the war. Poison **gas**, fighter planes and **tanks** are well-known examples, but less well known are the developments in reconstructive and prosthetic surgery. For Britain, the war created a legacy of an estimated 41,000 men who had lost limbs and 20,000 suffering facial wounds. Queen Mary's Convalescent Auxiliary Hospital in Roehampton, south-west of London, became a specialised orthopaedic hospital, with workshops serving an increasing demand for custom-made limbs. In 1916 Francis Derwent Wood founded The 3rd London General Hospital's Masks for Facial Disfigurement Department, which focused on facial prosthetics; soldiers nicknamed it 'The Tin Noses Shop'. The process was relatively simple. Plaster casts were taken of the patient's face, the wounded area 'rebuilt' and then the mask was made using galvanised copper and usually held on by spectacles. In the final stage the mask was painted by artists while the soldier was wearing it, in order to achieve the best skin-colour match possible. From 1917 at the main Queen's Hospital, in Kent, the surgeon Harold Gillies worked with artists, too, to create a prosthetic mask that could be worn over a facial injury. He dealt with many thousands of patients, and in 1920 he published *Plastic Surgery of the Face*, a pioneering work in this new discipline. Restoring a soldier's face or limb was not a vanity project. It was an attempt to assimilate the soldier back into civilian life by making his appearance more 'acceptable' to a society that might otherwise react adversely. Indeed, park benches close to Gillies' hospital were painted blue, to warn that any convalescent patient sitting there (in his hospital-blue uniform) might prove an upsetting sight.

KG

Q-SHIPS

Q-SHIPS

'Q-ships' were a creative British response to the **U-boat** threat. They were heavily armed merchant vessels, cunningly disguised to resemble vulnerable supply ships. Their efficacy relied on U-boats following the agreed rules of engagement of the time, which meant they needed to surface and warn the target ship's crew to evacuate before firing. But at this point a Q-ship would reveal a deck gun and turn the tables on its attacker. Named after their home port of Queenstown in Ireland, Q-ships were one of the best kept secrets of the war. They became a bugbear to the German Navy, which called these shadowy vessels *U-Boot-Fallen* (U-boat traps). Successful to a point, more and more Q-ships were being lost as the Germans got wiser to them, and eventually the Admiralty felt they could not justify the effort and manpower. One surviving Q-ship is HMS *President*, which can be found moored on the River Thames.

cs

RATIONING *to*
RUSSIA

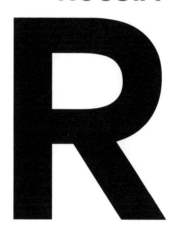

RATIONING

Compulsory rationing commenced in the UK in early 1918, when the impact of steadily rising prices and food shortages as a result of war became untenable. Despite the government's introduction of a voluntary code of rationing in 1917, queues for food became a near permanent fixture of the British high street as the war took men and **horses** away from farm work and reduced agricultural output, forced up prices and encouraged hoarding. Germany's unrestricted submarine warfare (*see* **U-boats**), designed to expose Britain to a food crisis by targeting its imports, led to the Ministry of Food finally establishing a rationing system for meat, butter and margarine in February 1918 in the London area; in July it was expanded nationally. Effective and successful, it both lessened the need to queue and ensured equality of food distribution. Other nations met the threat of food shortages less successfully. In **Russia** and **Turkey** the distribution of food broke down; indeed, the Russian Revolution in February 1917 had its origins in urban food riots, while in Turkey and **Austria-Hungary** many starved. In **Germany**, suffering under Britain's naval blockade, controls on food production and sale were badly devised and executed. While the German Army ensured that its men were adequately fed, by 1917 this meant that it was consuming 70 per cent of Germany's officially available food while civilians became increasingly malnourished – a disparity that encouraged revolutionary thoughts.

EP

RATS

While the prevailing conditions of the **Western Front** were conducive to the sprouting of **poppies**, a much less welcome consequence was the profusion of rats. Discarded food tins and other debris littered areas around trenches. Toilet facilities were insalubrious – a pit, or perhaps just buckets. In addition to that, after periods of fighting, decaying bodies (and body parts) would linger for days, or sometimes be completely buried by shell explosions. All together, the environment proved ideal for rats to flourish. The two types that roamed the trenches were the brown rat (*Rattus norvegicus*) and the black rat (*Rattus rattus*), the former feared due to their ability to grow large – soldiers reported seeing brown rats the size of cats. They liked to tuck into the dead by burrowing and eating the eyes first. Although rats were sometimes accused of going after a wounded soldier, rarely did they attack the living.

LM

RECRUITMENT

All sides in the war tried to ensure an adequate supply of men for the front, but Britain's need to recruit was particularly acute. Britain's army was a small but professional body, and its recent conflicts had all been in a colonial context. Now it was facing a vastly more numerous German Army. A recruitment campaign began within days of war being declared, as **Kitchener** – a non-adherent of the 'over by Christmas' school – called for men aged 19–30 to join the Army. **Posters** appeared that urged enlistment on the basis of patriotic duty, the injustice done to **Belgium** and familial obligation, all under an effort administered by the Parliamentary Recruiting Committee. At first the recruitment campaign was very successful, and recruitment offices were overwhelmed, with an average of 33,000 men joining every day. Three weeks later Kitchener raised the age-limit to 35, and by the middle of September 1914 over 500,000 men had volunteered. Enabling men to join up and serve with their **Pals** also helped the cause. But it took time to equip and train these 'New Armies', and during 1914 and 1915 a large burden of manning the trench lines fell on troops from **India**. During 1916, with recruitment numbers dwindling, politicians finally agreed the need for **conscription**. Volunteer numbers were not the only thing to dwindle. At the beginning of the war, the Army required its recruits to be at least 5 feet 6 inches tall, with a minimum chest measurement of 35 inches. By May 1915 this had reduced to 5 feet 3 inches (as the age limit rose to 40), and in July 1915 the Army even agreed to the formation of 'Bantam' battalions composed of men between 5 feet and 5 feet 3 inches in height.

RG

RED BARON

Perhaps the most widely known **ace** in the history of military aviation, the Red Baron led a literally colourful career. The Baron – real name Manfred von Richthofen – was born in 1892 into an aristocratic Prussian family with strong military links. At the beginning of the war he served in a German cavalry regiment on both the Eastern and Western fronts. Frustrated by the lack of opportunities for cavalry actions, he transferred to the Army's Air Service where, after training in the relatively new field of aerial combat, he became a highly proficient pilot. By 14 January 1917 he had scored 16 'kills' and was awarded the *Pour le Mérite* as well as command of a squadron. It was at this point that he began to have his aircraft painted the distinctive red, which soon led to his famous nickname. He flew different red aircraft, although the one most closely identified with him was the Fokker Triplane DR.1, which he piloted from October 1917. By this time he had been promoted to commander of an entire wing and had become widely celebrated within Germany, even producing a (ghost-written) war autobiography, *The Red Battle Flyer*. In total he had 80 confirmed kills, making him the most successful ace of the war. It was on Sunday 21 April 1918 that he was shot down and

killed during a dogfight with Captain Roy Brown of the
Royal Air Force. There has been debate over who fired the
fatal shots (with a strong claim for ground fire from Australian-
held trenches); but either way the man was dead – though the
legend thrived.

MJP

REHABILITATION

The legacies of the war were many and various, but one of the
most visible was the number of battle-scarred men. As has been
said, 'For disabled men the war did not end in 1918. It was a long
and tragic serial lasting, for many, for a life time.' Over 20 million
men, from all the belligerent nations, had been severely wounded,
and at the end of the war 8 million ex-servicemen returned home
permanently disabled. Of those, 750,000 were British. One of
the first attempts at their rehabilitation was the founding in
1915, by Sir Arthur Pearson, of St Dunstan's hostel for the war-
blinded. He firmly believed that 'blindness could be overcome'
and should not be regarded as a state of permanent dependency,
so to this end St Dunstaners were given vocational training, as
well as encouragement to take part in sports such as swimming
and rowing. Another early charity was the Not Forgotten
Association, founded in 1919, which aimed to 'provide comfort,
cheer and entertainment for the wounded ex-servicemen still in
hospital'. Before December 1916, disabled ex-servicemen had to
rely on voluntary organisations for help; but that month the
Ministry of Pensions was established, to administer war pensions
but also to organise further treatment, training and employment
of disabled veterans. It was a slow process, however, and by 1922
only 13,000 disabled men had been trained under government
programmes. More successful was the King's National Roll
Scheme, whereby firms undertook to ensure that 5 per cent of

their workforce were disabled ex-servicemen: by that means, nearly 90,000 veterans found employment within a year.

TC

REMEMBRANCE

Our modern rituals of war remembrance date back to the 1914–1918 conflict and its great toll of life. Immediately following the **Armistice** there were scenes of great and exuberant rejoicing in Britain. These were sometimes reprised in later years – in 1925 the Vicar of St Martins-in-the-Fields was writing to *The Times* about a 'thoughtless and ill-conceived' Armistice Ball at the Albert Hall. But given the scale of the casualties and the sacrifice, there was a national sense of loss and grief, and a need for commemorations that were more solemn. One innovation was the two-minute silence, first conducted on Armistice Day 1919 at the request of King George V. Sir Edwin Lutyens designed a temporary 'cenotaph' for Peace Day, 1919, and the popularity of this simple but striking monument was such that a permanent Cenotaph replaced the wooden one in 1920. Another symbolic site was created with the interment of an anonymous dead serviceman in Westminster Abbey. In 1920 more than a million people filed past the flag-covered grave of this Unknown Warrior, the week before it was sealed. Today, both locations remain at the heart of remembrance of modern wars. Around the country, from etched panels in school halls to village **war memorials**, communities recorded the names of their dead. The actual remains of those dead invariably lay in some foreign field, and the Imperial (now Commonwealth) War Graves Commission undertook the task of establishing and maintaining permanent cemeteries and memorials across the world, becoming focal points for pilgrimages by presidents and ordinary people alike over the decades. At the Menin Gate near **Ypres**, and elsewhere, names of the many 'missing' were inscribed on monuments. Surviving veterans and their dependents were remembered too, and in 1921 several organisations combined into the (Royal) British Legion to co-ordinate charitable efforts for them, and artificial **poppies** were sold to raise funds, establishing that most visible symbol of remembrance.

FC

REPARATIONS

During the war, both the **Allies** and the **Central Powers** planned to exact financial and material vengeance when victory was finally won: reparations. With the signing of the **Armistice**, there was a popular expectation in Britain and **France** that Germany would be forced to pay for 'causing all the loss and damage' of the war and in doing so would be 'squeezed until the pips squeaked'. France, particularly, had a barely concealed desire to keep post-war **Germany** weakened for as long as possible. But at the 1919 Paris Peace Conference the question of how much Germany would pay was not satisfactorily resolved, and it was only in January 1921 that the Allied Supreme Council set a figure of $56 billion. This was reduced to $16 billion five months later, but Germany was both unwilling and unable to pay the annual instalments, and the ensuing default led to a Franco-Belgian occupation of the Ruhr industrial region. This was followed by the period of German hyper-inflation and economic collapse. An American plan helped solve the immediate problem of inflation but failed in providing a long-term solution. A later plan, devised by American financier Owen D. Young in 1929, put annual payments at $8 billion over the next 58.5 years. It was bitterly attacked by Hitler and the Nazis, but – given the world economic crisis in the Depression years – by the time they came to power in January 1933 Germany had already ceased paying reparations.

TC

ROYAL FLYING CORPS

The Royal Flying Corps (RFC) was the aviation branch of the British Army. Along with the Royal Naval Air Service, it grew from what was in 1914 little over a hundred multi-purpose **aeroplanes** to, by 1918, thousands of combat and support aircraft and over a quarter of a million personnel, all part of a new, merged, independent air arm: the Royal Air Force. The RFC's main, and most vital, jobs were reconnaissance and observing the fall of **artillery** shells to assist the gunners with their aim, though it soon developed into a force capable of attacking targets on the ground and pursuing the necessary 'dogfighting' for supremacy in the air. In the final **Hundred Days Offensive**, the RAF operated in close support of attacking infantry and tanks. Dominance over the **Western Front** see-sawed between the Allied air arms and the German Air Service as new **aeroplanes**, weapons and fighting techniques were developed. And although they were spared many of the horrors of the trenches, pilots and observers endured a brutal war in the air. It was no wonder that the exploits of **aces** such as Billy Bishop, 'Mick' Mannock, James McCudden and Albert Ball turned them into national heroes. The wood and fabric aircraft in which the airmen flew frequently caught fire, and the crews did not carry parachutes. In one particularly intense period of fighting in 1917, known as 'Bloody April', the life expectancy of new RFC pilots could be measured in weeks, with some surviving only a few days. 'The most difficult duty,' recalled one young squadron commander, 'was on the many occasions one had to write to the next of kin to advise them of the death or capture of their sons. That was a horrifying thing for a boy of twenty-one to have to do.'

CW

ROYAL NAVY

In August 1914, Britain's Navy had 'ruled the waves' almost unchallenged since the Battle of Trafalgar in 1805. In the First World War – despite occasional startling reverses and the loss of 35,000 men, 13 battleships, 3 battle-cruisers, 25 cruisers, 67 destroyers and 54 submarines – it continued to do so. Only once, at **Jutland** in 1916, was its supremacy even remotely challenged. Even then, and despite suffering greater losses than the Germans, Britain's Grand Fleet (protecting the home waters) was ready again for action within a day, while its opponent was crippled and confined to port for many months. At the beginning of the war, the Royal Navy had set about sweeping German naval and merchant ships from the seas and oceans, a task effectively completed by March 1915, after which German ships were effectively locked into the North Sea. Naval victories were won at Heligoland Bight (August 1914), at the Battle of the Falklands (December 1914, where the German East Asiatic Squadron was largely destroyed), and at Dogger Bank (January 1915). There had been German successes – the battlecruiser *Emden*'s targets of opportunity in the Pacific, the bombardment of East Coast British towns (November and December 1914), and the humiliating destruction of Sir Christopher Craddock's squadron off the coast of Chile (at the Battle of Coronel, November 1914). But these were little more than dents to British prestige. The **U-boat** threat was genuine, and genuinely feared; but, after some anxious months in 1917, that was effectively mastered too. Yet the Royal Navy's greatest achievement on 'the trenchless sea', and one largely unnoticed and unsung at the time – and since – was the blockade that effectively strangled Germany's war economy. In King George V's words, the Royal Navy had proved 'once again the sure shield of Britain and her Empire in the hour of trial'.

TC

RUSSIA

Only nine years before August 1914, Russia had suffered a humiliating defeat in its war with Japan. At the same time a revolution had forced the charming but weak and stubborn Tsar Nicholas II to make some concessions towards constitutional government. Now, war with Germany seemed to offer the regime an opportunity to redeem itself, and in 1914 a wave of patriotic, almost mystical, fervour gripped the country, especially in the big cities. To improve efficiency both in mobilisation and production, vodka and other spirits were banned. At first all seemed to go well as the Russian 'steamroller' invaded East Prussia. But within weeks, defeats by the Germans at **Tannenberg** and the Masurian Lakes set a trend. Russia fared better against **Austria-Hungary**, and both sides experienced their ups and downs on the fickle **Eastern Front**. But in 1915 the Russians were in full-scale retreat. The Tsar replaced his uncle Grand Duke Nicholas as commander-in-chief – with himself – in September 1915, but continuing Russian defeats only increased his unpopularity. His wife Alexandra, thought to be pro-German, was openly detested. The achievements of General **Brusilov** in 1916 offered an opportunity for better success, but circumstances and Russia's underlying weaknesses meant it was too late. The Army was chronically short of arms and ammunition, and on the home front there were food shortages and continual breakdowns in the transport system. The government was in chaos with four different prime ministers in a year. Things came to a head in March 1917 when strikes and riots broke out in the capital, Petrograd (St Petersburg). Soldiers, ordered to fire on the rioters, instead sided with them. On 13 March (28 February by Russia's Gregorian calendar), Nicholas abdicated, and by the end of the year the Bolsheviks under Lenin had seized power – and declared a unilateral armistice. Russia's war had seen an

THE FIRST WORLD WAR A–Z

astonishing 12 million men mobilised, of whom over 9 million became casualties, including 1.7 million dead. By March 1918, Bolshevik Russia was definitively out of the war, giving up vast territories for peace in the Treaty of Brest-Litovsk. An era ended on 16 July 1918, as Nicholas and his family were shot to death on Bolshevik orders.

TC & KG

SALONIKA *to* SYKES–PICOT

SALONIKA

The Salonika (or Macedonian) Front was much argued over at
the time, and afterwards, for seeming to suck in large quantities
of Allied men and supplies to little avail. It began in October
1915, when British and French troops landed in neutral Greece
to try and prevent Bulgaria joining with **Germany** and
Austria-Hungary to crush **Serbia**. The Allies failed, but their
armies – under overall French command – remained in Greece,
manning a line north of the port of Salonika (Thessaloniki), their
main supply base. For months, little seemed to happen – though
in November Serbs achieved a morale-boosting recapture of their
city of Monastir (Bitola) – and Allied politicians and generals
questioned whether to keep the front open. Yet by 1917, 500,000
Allied troops, in six national contingents, faced 300,000 men
from all *four* **Central Powers**, along a front line stretching from
Albania to the mouth of the River Struma in Greece. The British
Salonika Force (BSF) under General George Milne held some
ninety miles of it in the east, including the key strategic position
at Doiran. A major Allied offensive in April 1917, which also
involved Italians and Russians, failed and static trench warfare
continued until autumn 1918. Throughout, the living conditions
for both sides were harsh; winter and summer brought extremes
of climate, and disease, especially malaria, caused many more
casualties than fighting. Everything changed on 15 September
1918, when Allied forces directed by General Louis Franchet
d'Esperey – 'Desperate Frankie' as the Tommies dubbed him
– went onto the offensive. The BSF with Greek support (Greece
having formally joined the Allies in June 1917) attacked at Doiran,
helping the French and Serbs break the Bulgarian defences. The
Bulgarian Army was forced into a comprehensive retreat, and on
29 September Bulgaria became the first of the Central Powers to
throw in the towel and agree an armistice.

AW

SCHLIEFFEN PLAN

Amid the tense geopolitics of Europe before 1914, **Germany** had always anticipated some future war with **France**, a country for which defeat and loss of territory in the Franco-Prussian War (1870–1871) still rankled. Moreover, France's **Entente** with **Russia** meant that Germany would most likely be faced by enemies to the east and west. In such a climate, the so-called Schlieffen Plan developed – Germany's war plan and the brainchild of Count Alfred von Schlieffen, the professional head of the German Army for 15 years until his retirement in 1906. The original plan, approved in 1899, allowed for a lightning campaign against France while Russia was still mobilising. Schlieffen believed that a *direct* attack on France would prove unsuccessful, so he planned to strike north with his right wing through neutral **Belgium**, in massive strength, and then swoop down around Paris, taking the French from the rear. Once France had been quickly defeated, Germany's main effort could be transferred to its eastern borders, which at first would be only lightly defended. In the event, when war broke out, Schlieffen's supposed last words 'to keep the right wing strong' were ignored by his successor Helmuth von Moltke. He reduced its strength to face a build-up of French forces along the whole frontier. But Moltke's action, although the most important, was just one factor that led to the final failure of the plan, on the **Marne**. The unexpected resistance of the Belgians under King Albert, Britain's prompt dispatch of the **BEF**, the Germans' logistical stretch and the failures of German commanders in the field, as well as the speed at which the Russians mobilised and invaded East Prussia – all played their part. Summing up Schlieffen's plan, historian A J P Taylor's verdict was: 'He would be content with nothing less than total victory; therefore he exposed Germany to total defeat.'

TC

SCRAP OF PAPER

On 4 August 1914, Britain declared war on **Germany** because its troops had violated neutral Belgian territory in their bid to deliver a decisive blow against **France**, as envisaged in the **Schlieffen Plan**. That evening, the British Ambassador in Berlin, Sir Edward Goschen, met German Chancellor Theobald von Bethmann-Hollweg in order to receive his passport so he could leave what was fast becoming an enemy country. During the conversation Bethmann-Hollweg expressed his amazement that Britain would go to war over 'a scrap of paper', referring to the 1839 Treaty of London, whereby Britain, Germany and other European powers had pledged to guarantee the independence and neutrality of **Belgium**. His clumsy words seemed to reflect the utter disregard of the German **Kaiser** and his government and military for any treaties or international law, and to signal a blunt belief that 'might is right'. For British **propaganda**, the phrases 'scrap of paper' and 'might is right' became valuable and often-used slogans in the effort to mobilise the British public for the war effort and to win over public opinion in neutral nations, above all the **United States**.

MS

SERBIA

'The Serbs deserve a good thrashing' was **Asquith**'s opinion following the **assassination** of Archduke Franz Ferdinand at the hands of a Serbian-inspired nationalist. It was a view shared by many in Britain, who saw the Balkan kingdom as a semi-barbarous country; it had brutally murdered its own king and queen in 1903, after all. But once war came, Serbia was second only to **Belgium** as an object of British sympathy. **Austria-Hungary's** attempts to invade the country were successfully repulsed in 1914, but at a cost of over 170,000

Serbian casualties. The following year, the Austro-Hungarians, now joined by the Germans and Bulgarians, achieved better success. The Serbian Army and government, together with thousands of refugees, were forced to retreat, at a cost of 140,000 lives, over the Albanian mountains. After regrouping on Corfu, the remnants of the Serbian Army went back into action on the **Salonika** Front in 1916, recapturing the city of Bitola on 29 November. The exit of **Russia** from the war in 1917 saw Serbia lose its principal supporter among the Allies, and there were fears too of Italian encroachments on Serbian territory. When the Serbian Army re-entered the country following the Bulgarian collapse in September 1918, it found a devastated land. The occupation by the **Central Powers** had been a brutal one, and a rebellion in the Toplica region during early 1917 had been put down with the loss of 20,000 lives. It is estimated that 25 per cent of Serbia's population, around 1.2 million people, were killed or died of starvation and disease as a result of the war. It was, proportionally, the heaviest toll of any combatant nation.

TC

SHELL SHOCK

As soon as the fighting began, a significant number of soldiers began to show symptoms of sensory loss and mental breakdown, experiencing acute depression and nightmares. Extreme symptoms could include paralysis or loss of speech. At first, medical opinion believed that the physical force of a shell explosion was the origin of this 'shell shock'. But servicemen who had never been under shell fire also began experiencing the symptoms. Gradually, psychologists recognised that the cause of shell shock, or 'neurasthenia', was the emotional disturbance produced by the wider conditions of war. Conflict between the natural instinct of self-preservation and the consequences, both military and social, of fleeing from danger meant that shell shock was often a form of psychological escape from a seemingly intolerable situation. Shell shock was usually treated with a combination of bed rest and regimental drill. More acute cases were hospitalised and subjected to disciplinary therapy. Treatment emphasised the need for a quick cure, sometimes even involving humiliation or pain, including the application of electric shocks to stimulate nerves. (Electric-shock treatment was also deemed successful for weeding out malingerers.) Therapy for officers tended to lean towards psychotherapy, using conversation and hypnosis to allow the patient to confront his repressed trauma. Shell shock remained a serious problem following demobilisation. By one estimate for Britain in 1920, 65,000 people were drawing disability pensions for war-related mental disorders, of which 9,000 were still undergoing medical treatment. It was not until the 1980s, though, that Post-Traumatic Stress Disorder (PTSD) – the condition that includes what was once called 'shell shock' – was recognised as a distinct malady.

AR

SLANG

Military slang abounded in the war, and the British Army and Navy – with their rich imperial heritage – had a broad seam to draw on. Hindustani (Hindi) gave **Blighty** and *khaki*, along with *pukkah* meaning 'real' or 'proper' and *burgoo*, meaning 'porridge'. Soldiers had their own customised versions of rhyming slang too, so, for example, *babbling brook* was a 'cook', *France and Spain* was 'rain' and *Uncle Ned* referred to 'bed'. There were inter-service variations, so, for example, soldiers had *buckshee* for something that was free of charge, while sailors used the term *Harry Freeman's*. Interestingly, *swaddy*, to describe a British soldier, was originally a sailor's term; it caught on and was used throughout the war by soldiers too, until its spelling changed to *squaddie* some time during the Second World War. Servicemen had slang for every conceivable aspect of their experiences. The ammunition hurled at them acquired its familiar turns of phrase, so that a 77mm shell was a *whizz-bang* and a German stick grenade was a *potato masher*; in return, the British threw *pineapples* (Mills bomb grenades) and *plum puddings* (trench mortar shells). The best-known slang, though, was that used to describe the enemy and the sometimes unpronounceable places in which the squaddies found themselves. The Germans were *Fritz* or – as much favoured in propaganda – the merciless **Hun**. But they could also be the *Boche* or even the *Alleyman*, both derived from the French. ('Take me over the sea, / where the Alleyman can't get at me', as one trench song had it). **Ypres** was *Wipers*, Montaubon was *Monty Bong,* and the Flemish town of Poperinghe, where soldiers often rested out of the line, was – mercifully – just *Pop.*

GJ

SOMME

In British remembrance of the war, 'the Somme' has a resonance like no other name, and for two reasons. Almost 20,000 died on its first day, out of nearly 60,000 British and Imperial casualties – still the biggest British military loss on any single day. And the campaign seemed to symbolise the futility and waste of the war, its stalemate and pointless attrition. Ironically, this area of Picardy, where the Somme and Ancre rivers meet, was known earlier in the war as one of the quieter sections of the front line. Only after an unsuccessful year for the British, which saw them pushed back at **Ypres** in 1915, and the Franco-German bloodletting at **Verdun** from February 1916, was the Somme agreed on by Allied commanders as the place for a large-scale offensive. It was where the British and French portions of the line met, and one major goal was to force the Germans to switch troops away from Verdun. The campaign started with a two-week long bombardment, designed to decimate German lines. It largely failed in this regard, as well as giving away the element of surprise. The infantry assault commenced on 1 July 1916, and thousands of the men who had answered Kitchener's call for volunteers now approached the enemy lines, many of them at walking speed as instructed. Many barely made it more than a few yards beyond their trenches. In terms of objectives gained, there were successes – for the Canadians and (especially) the French – but they were clouded by the dawning reality among British commanders of the cost. Fighting continued for months – attacks and counter-attacks – with all sides suffering heavy losses, and in September the British sought to gain the upper hand with their new machine of war: the **tank**. In November 1916, the campaign finally ended. The prolonged struggle turned raw recruits into battle-hardened soldiers, provided the British Army with the opportunity to experiment with tactics, and was arguably an important part of the Allies' 'learning curve'. And they had advanced 6 miles, the farthest advance of the war since 1914. Against this must be counted the enormous human cost. Those territorial gains were temporarily lost in spring 1918; but at the Second Battle of the Somme, in August 1918, the Allies succeeded in driving the Germans into a lasting retreat.

EC

SONGS

Songs of all kinds were popular in the war, on the home and fighting fronts – to boost morale, to reassure with something familiar, as vehicles for **propaganda** or irreverent humour, and sometimes to pluck the heartstrings. Sailors had their sea shanties, and soldiers had their marching songs. In Britain, people could send postcards bearing the words and music to popular songs, and often showing a sentimental or patriotic scene in the background. Some individual songs entered the culture. 'Pack up Your Troubles in Your Old Kit Bag', a marching song written in 1915, has come to characterise the **Tommy**. Equally famous is 'It's a Long Way to Tipperary': soldiers singing it were overheard by a newspaper correspondent in Boulogne, in August 1914, and it was popularised and taken up by civilians too. But naval and military songs usually took hymns, traditional ballads or music-hall songs and changed – or subverted – their words to match the men's experiences, from the wistful to the darkly humorous to the effusively vulgar. Thus, 'No more sergeants bawling "Pick it up" and "Put it down" / If I meet the ugly bastard I'll kick his arse all over town' was sung to the tune of 'What a Friend We Have in Jesus'. The period's songs had a new lease of life with the production of *Oh! What a Lovely War* in 1963.

GJ

SPIES

Then, as now, spies were both feared and fascinating, as the novels of John Buchan demonstrated, and the war produced one of the most famous (alleged) spies in the annals of espionage: **Mata Hari**. In Britain a concern with secrecy preceded the war, on account of the tense Anglo-German naval rivalry, and the result was the creation in 1909 of a new Secret Service Bureau, with both Home and Foreign sections that in due course became better known as MI5 and MI6. With war declared, the new **DORA** legislation made passing information to the enemy punishable by death. Gustav Steinhauer, a German naval officer, took part in espionage in pre-war Britain. His letters were intercepted by MI5, and he escaped back to Germany in 1914, later producing a memoir of his exploits. In fact, enemy spying in

Britain was not well organised and on a small scale: 120 German spies came to Britain, and 65 were arrested, 19 of whom were sentenced to death; others drifted back home. The first to die, in November 1914, was Carl Hans Lody, who had the dubious honour of the first execution at the Tower of London for 150 years. Nevertheless, MI5 found itself swamped with reports of possible spies by concerned members of the public, and its staffing increased from just over 50 in 1914 to 844 in 1918. MI5's activities were aided by a huge **letter**-opening operation at the Post Office and the internment of over 4,000 'enemy aliens'. One of its greatest successes came after the secret execution of spy Karl Muller (July 1915), when operatives continued to send bogus information back to Germany, forging Muller's handwriting and using his technique of lemon juice as invisible ink. Times, though, were changing. Technology, in the form of decoded signals and aerial photography, were already beginning to redefine spying.

sc

SYKES–PICOT

The shape of the Middle East today owes much to two Allied diplomats, Britain's Sir Mark Sykes and France's François-Georges-Picot. In May 1916, they produced a secret agreement intended to divide the bulk of the Ottoman Empire, after **Turkey**'s defeat, between Britain and France. This would consist of British (red) and French (blue) zones of 'direct or indirect administration of control'. Although the agreement paid lip-service to the establishment of 'an independent Arab state or a confederation of Arab states', it was clear that the two Allied powers would have the whip hand in any such arrangement. The Sykes–Picot Agreement flew in the face of promises made to the Arabs by T E **Lawrence** and others of an independent state with Damascus – which was earmarked for France by the terms of the agreement – as its capital. Because of its interests along Turkey's north-eastern border, Tsarist Russia became a silent partner to the agreement; but after the Bolsheviks seized power in November 1917, they publicised its contents, much to the embarrassment of Britain and France. In 1920 the Treaty of Sèvres divided up Turkey's empire very much along the lines of the Sykes–Picot Agreement. Instead of outright colonization, Britain and France assumed League of Nations mandates over Turkey's former Middle Eastern territories. Syria, which then included present-day Lebanon, went to France, while Jordan, Iraq, Palestine and the Gulf States came under British tutelage. In essence, the map of the modern Middle East was drawn up, although it was not until 1948 that the state of Israel would emerge. But its creation had been foreseen by another document from the First World War, the November 1917 **Balfour Declaration**.

TC

TALISMAN *to* TURKEY

TALISMAN

In times of crisis, people have often put their trust in symbolic objects that might confer protection or bring reassurance. In 1914, many soldiers travelled to the front carrying good-luck charms, often given to them by loved ones. Once at the front men saw that death could often be arbitrary and survival random, so these treasured objects provided comfort in the face of uncertainties. Talisman ranged from an amber heart to protect against drowning, to silver 'fumsup' charms (a play on 'thumbs up'), popular with the Royal Flying Corps. A 'soldier's farthing', sewn into clothing near the heart, was believed to bestow divine intervention on the wearer. Superstitions were not restricted to the front, however. In Paris, 'Nenette and Rintintin' woollen doll **mascots** were widely believed to provide protection against German air raids. (A number of these charms and amulets are now in IWM's collections.) One did not even need to be religious or superstitious to appreciate talismen. Edward Lovett, a collector of amulets, was dismissive of their magical properties; but he still made his younger son take one to the front.

NW

TANKS

One piece of British technical innovation was to have a transformative effect on the way future wars would be fought: the tank. It was an advance pioneered, perhaps surprisingly, by the **Royal Navy**. In 1915 **Churchill**, in his capacity as First Lord of the Admiralty, formed the 'Landship Committee', which commissioned William Foster and Co. Ltd to design a vehicle that would break the deadlock of trench warfare. As a result, Major Walter Wilson and Sir William Tritton came up with the first landship from pieces of agricultural equipment. Originally called the 'Number I Lincoln Machine', it became known as

Little Willie, an insult to the **Kaiser**. Further developments, to enable the machine to get across trenches and to add firepower, produced the prototype of the Mark I version – *Mother*. When it was unveiled to **Lloyd George**, in February 1916, he enthused: 'at last we have the answer to the German machine guns and wire'. To keep landships a secret, everyone was told that they were actually mobile water tanks for **Mesopotamia**, and hence the designation 'tank'. They were unleashed on the battlefield on 15 September 1916, at the Battle of Flers-Courcelette, during the **Somme** campaign. They did not – yet – fulfil Lloyd George's hopes and had numerous technical problems; but the lumbering giants so intimidated the Germans that General **Haig** immediately ordered 100 more. Tanks underwent continual development, in both their 'male' forms (with 6-pounder guns) and 'female' forms (with machine guns), and by the summer of 1918 they were a regular component of the British arsenal. Tritton's reward, though, for transforming the face of warfare was a modest 33 shillings (£1.65) per tank.

RH

TANNENBERG

The Battle of Tannenburg (23–30 August 1914) was one of the first battles of the war and a decisive German victory over **Russia**. In August 1914 the Russian General Staff were keen to take the war to **Germany** as quickly as possible. At the urging of **France**, they assembled two armies and invaded East Prussia, the most vulnerable German province to Russian attack. The Germans were surprised by the speed of the Russian advance. They carried out an uncoordinated counter-attack with their Eigth Army, at Gumbinnen, and were forced to fall back, leaving East Prussia at risk of being overrun and generating panic in Germany. The ineffectual commander of the Eigth Army was sacked and replaced with the retired **Hindenburg** along with **Ludendorff**, hero of the siege of Liège in **Belgium**. Aided by aerial reconnaissance and signals intercepts, which showed that the two Russian armies were diverging, Ludendorff carried out an audacious plan to isolate one of them. He split his own forces, including transporting two corps quickly south by rail to attack the flank of the Russian Second Army. The Germans inflicted a crushing defeat. The Russians sustained an estimated 168,000 casualties, the majority falling prisoner; the Russian Second Army was completely annihilated. Unable to face the shame of the dawning defeat, its commander Samsonov took his own life. Ludendorff, by contrast, was ecstatic, recording in his memoirs: 'The battle was a glorious triumph for the generals and their troops [...] even now when I think of Liège and Tannenberg, my heart swells with pardonable satisfaction.'

RWR

TOMMY

Although the nickname 'Tommy' for the stereotypical British soldier has a long lineage, it is particularly associated with the First World War. It is, in fact, an abbreviation of 'Tommy Atkins'. The exact origin of the term is unclear, but it was in use from at least the 1800s. Its first appearance in an official publication was in 1815, when War Office guidance used the name 'Tommy Atkins' as an example of how a soldier's pocket book should be filled out. And so it acquired its generic association – though Irish, Scottish and Welsh soldiers tended to regard it as an English term and would take exception at being called a 'Tommy'.

PS

TOTAL WAR

The First World War has often been described as a 'total war', in which whole populations geared themselves up to defeat their opponents. According to the definition, in a total war civilians and the military work tirelessly, and often willingly, to aid their nation's military struggle, a struggle that often has far-reaching war aims. At home, their support might present itself in many different ways, as it did in 1914–1918: toiling in the **munitions** factories or down the mines, volunteering for work on farms or in hospitals, joining the home-defence organisations, and, importantly, by accepting privations (such as **rationing**) and limits to liberty, and in Britain by accepting the novelty of **conscription**. While a country on a total-war footing puts enormous effort into such universal participation, it can also turn civilians into – arguably legitimate – targets for attack, as demonstrated, for example, in the German air raids on England. Throughout the First World War, all the major participants experienced aspects of total war. In Britain, the suffragettes suspended their militant protests, **Ireland**'s Home Rule was put on hold, **women** replaced men in the factories and other workplaces, and production and skills were re-orientated towards the war. And, of course, men enlisted in their millions for a war that consumed millions. It has been asserted that people's willingness, ultimately, to accept the conditions of total war is what enabled the war's duration, its global scope, and the sheer level of ferocity it attained.

PWD

TOYS

Toy-making did not stop when war broke out; indeed, the war generated a whole new market, and children were generally spoilt for choice when it came to war-themed toys and games. In Britain they might play *Wartime Happy Families*, with cards portraying 'Lucy Atkins the Soldier's Daughter', or indulge in a game of *Trench Football*, or admire dolls and figures of patriotic personalities such as **Kitchener**. Such toys were marketed as being British-made and British-designed, to push home the patriotic message (and to increase sales), and they encouraged children to engage with the war from an early age. Soldiers made toys, too, for personal and patriotic purposes. Injured soldiers at convalescent hospitals across Britain were employed in toy-making as part of their rehabilitation: from a health point of view, the machinery could help in building up wasted muscle – and wounded soldiers still able to provide for their country was an uplifting message to convey. No less creatively-minded, German and Turkish **POWs** also made toys, including beaded snakes and animal or human figures, created with their loved ones in mind or simply as a means to keep occupied.

KC

TRENCH JOURNALS

The trench journal, many examples of which are in the collections of IWM, was one of the relatively few light-hearted features of the war. Many British infantry battalions and artillery batteries, engineers and service companies, ambulance trains and cavalry squadrons, regularly brought out their own magazines. They were often produced in difficult and dangerous conditions and by soldiers who, as a rule, knew little or nothing about journalism. Nevertheless, many achieved a high standard, and they often provided an initial forum for those like F W Harvey in the *Fifth Gloucester Gazette* and Gilbert Frankau in the *Wipers Times* who went on to have distinguished literary careers. The impulse behind the trench journal was, more often than not, to give a very disparate group of citizen soldiers a sense of *esprit de corps*. They also acted as a safety valve for the vast army of those citizen soldiers confronted by a strange new world of military life and discipline. Today, for us, the value of trench journals lies in the fact that they are one of the few places where the authentic voice of the ordinary soldier can be heard. And the voice we hear is one of fortitude, humour, intelligence, dignity and, most importantly, of casual insubordination.

TC

TRENCHES

Without doubt, the trench is the most potent, enduring and iconic image of the war. Trenches had figured prominently in the American Civil War of 1861–1865 and the more recent Russo-Japanese War of 1904–1905. But it was between 1914 and 1918 that the trench became such a dominating feature of the battlefield, especially on the **Western Front**, defining the routines of a soldier's life and the nature of battle. Before 1914, neither the Allies nor the Germans had anticipated or planned for static warfare. But by the autumn of 1914, firepower, especially **artillery**, had gained the upper hand over manoeuvre, and the result was lines of opposing, defensive trenches, separated by **no man's land**. On the Western Front, trenches were normally slightly deeper than a soldier's height, with a fire-step built into the forward wall, which allowed defenders to deploy their rifles and light **machine guns** in the event of an enemy attack. The bottoms of the trenches were covered with duckboards – wooden slats – to keep the men out of the mud and water that inevitably flooded the trenches, especially on the wet Flanders Plain. Trenches were reinforced with wooden beams and sandbags to prevent them from collapsing under shell fire. By 1916, the standard British trench system consisted of a front-line trench, usually zig-zagged to give a maximum field of fire, a support trench and a reserve trench in the rear. As defenders, determined to hang on to their occupied territory, the Germans had better-constructed, more permanent-looking trenches than the British or French, and they used concrete to fortify strongpoints and underground shelters.

TC

TUNNELLING

A celebrated sequence from the contemporary documentary
film *The Battle of the Somme* shows an enormous mine being
detonated under the German trenches on Hawthorn Ridge, as
battle commences. It was but one product of the intensive
tunnelling that both sides carried out on the **Western Front**, in
response to a war of **trenches**. The largest and most effective use
of mines was on 7 June 1917, when 19 British mines were exploded
at **Messines**, with a force so powerful that the blasts were
reportedly heard in London. Today, such craters are still visible,
and in some cases the ground still encases unexploded mines.
The main impetus for tunnelling, though, was defensive – to
protect one's own lines from the hostile tunnelling of the enemy.
Men from Britain and the Empire with specialist skills were
recruited for the job, including miners, engineers and even sewer
builders who had developed a method of 'clay kicking' ideally
suited to the heavy soils of Flanders. Tunnels could take up to a
year to complete, with the men working in the cramped, dark
conditions and in near silence for fear of discovery and an
unpleasant death. The result was a highly hazardous war of
nerves, as groups of tunnellers worked as quietly as possible,
constantly checking with their listening devices for signs of the
enemy, and sometimes detonating charges to blow in enemy
tunnels and bury alive the enemy tunnellers.

cc

TURKEY

The Ottoman Empire, often just referred to as Turkey, had been
the medieval superpower, its vast territory covering much of
Eastern Europe, North **Africa** and the Middle East. But by 1914 it
was long regarded as 'the sick man of Europe'. A shadow of its
former self, it was deeply in debt, challenged by neighbours such as

Russia, beset by internal weaknesses and divisions, and much smaller in size, its hold over the Balkans now vanished. Prior to the start of the war, the Turks had attempted to forge closer links with Britain, **France** and **Russia**, but received little enthusiasm for their efforts. Better luck was had with **Germany**, whose **Kaiser** seems to have been much more sympathetic, resulting in a secret alliance in 1914. When war broke out, Turkey remained technically neutral; but on 2 August 1914 the pro-German and pro-war faction of 'Young Turks' in the Turkish Cabinet had already signed a secret alliance with Germany, and by November the country had joined the **Central Powers**. Its entry into war began with a bombardment of Russia's Black Sea ports on 29 October 1914. Seven days later Britain and France declared war on Turkey and on 14 November the Sultan proclaimed a holy war (*Jihad*) against the **Allies**. Turkey fended off the Allied attempt to seize the Dardanelles Straits during the **Gallipoli** campaign of 1915–1916, but with huge losses. Otherwise, despite the fact that much of the military direction was under German control, Turkish victories were few, costly and temporary, and the Muslim subjects of the Allies' empires did generally not – as hoped – rise up. Instead, Arabs (under T E **Lawrence** and Prince Feisal) rebelled against Ottoman rule, and the British and Imperial forces made their way north through **Palestine** and **Mesopotamia**, taking Jerusalem, Damascus and Baghdad. Turkey's war ended on 30 October 1918 with the Armistice of Moudros, and with it came Allied occupation and soon the loss of all the empire's territory beyond Turkey, as per the **Sykes-Picot** agreement. The 1920 Treaty of Sèvres gave large areas of territory to Greece, which led Turkish nationalists, under war hero Mustafa Kemal ('Atatürk'), to fight and defeat the Greeks in a war of independence, expelling them and the remaining Allied occupiers in 1922. In 1923 the modern state of Turkey, moulded by Atatürk, formally replaced the Ottoman Empire.

CM

U-BOATS *to* UNITED STATES

U-BOATS

Germany's use of submarines to target merchant ships was a major development of the war. The U-boat (*Unterseeboot*) campaign began with the sinking of the first British merchant ship, the SS *Giltra*, in October 1914 and continued until the **Armistice**. For the first six months of the war Germany obeyed the so-called 'Prize Rules', whereby U-boats surfaced and allowed crew and passengers to leave a vessel before sinking it with gunfire. But in February 1915 Germany declared the seas around Britain a 'war zone' within which merchant ships, including those from neutral countries, would be sunk without warning. This 'unrestricted submarine warfare' was intended to blockade Britain, which was already using the **Royal Navy** to blockade Germany. Following the controversial sinking of RMS *Lusitania* in May 1915, Germany briefly abandoned its policy in response to pressure from the **United States** and other neutral countries. However, after the Battle of **Jutland** a year later, Germany resumed unrestricted submarine warfare, and Britain became alarmed at the rising losses. The sinking of 500 supply-carrying ships between February and April 1917 alone spurred British moves to introduce **rationing** in 1918. But Germany paid a severe price, in that submarine warfare became a prime reason for US entry into the war. British methods to counter submarines were limited but became increasingly effective, notably the introduction of escorted convoys in June 1917, the use of dazzle **camouflage** and specific anti-submarine weapons such as depth charges. There was also the British ruse of disguised **Q-ships**. By the **Armistice** in 1918, the submarine threat had been neutralised.

IP

UNITED STATES

When war broke out in August 1914, the almost universal reaction in the United States was summed up by a Chicago newspaper: 'Peace loving citizens of this country will now rise and tender a hearty vote of thanks to Columbus for having discovered America.' President **Wilson** called on Americans to be neutral 'in word and thought' and the New York *World* opined: 'If Europe insists on committing suicide, Europe must furnish for Europe's funeral.' But strict neutrality was an impossibility, and the war came forcibly home to America when the *Lusitania* was sunk in May 1915 with the loss of 128 US citizens. Yet Wilson's reaction, to the disgust of many Americans, including former and future presidents Theodore and Franklin D. Roosevelt, was to speak of being 'too proud to fight'. In November 1916 he was narrowly re-elected as 'The Man Who Kept Us Out of the War'. But just three months later German **U-boats** resumed unrestricted submarine warfare and in February 1917 the United States severed diplomatic relations with **Germany**. At the end of the month, the contents of the inflammatory **Zimmermann telegram** became public. On 2 April Wilson finally asked Congress for a declaration of war, affirming that 'the world must be made safe for democracy'. With a small army, the United States could not immediately tip the scales of war. But the promise of its immense resources and pool of manpower would alter everyone's thinking and decision-making. The first US units on the **Western Front** fought with borrowed weapons, borrowed uniforms, and under French or British command. But in June 1918 US divisions contributed significantly to the Second Battle of the **Marne**, and by August 1918 two armies of the American Expeditionary Force were in the field.

TC

VERDUN *to*
VICTORIA CROSS

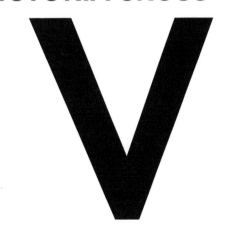

VADs *see* NURSES

VERDUN

The titanic ten-month Battle of Verdun scarred the French nation as deeply as the **Somme** did Britain. On 21 February 1916, the German Army launched a thunderous assault on the forts defending the historic French town. Whether intended as a breakthrough, or as a deliberate attempt to 'bleed to death' the French Army as it sacrificed more and more men to Verdun's defence (as German commander Falkenhayn later claimed was the intention), it was the beginning of the longest and bloodiest battle of the war. That Verdun was not lost owes much to General **Pétain**, drafted in at the moment of crisis to direct the defence. He depended almost exclusively on a narrow supply road dubbed *la Voie Sacrée* (the Sacred Way), which regularly rotated French troops into and out of Verdun. The French spirit of defiance was summed up in the slogans associated with Pétain and Verdun: *Ils ne passeront pas!'* ('They shall not pass!') and *'On les aura!'* ('We'll get 'em!'). With collapse averted, General Robert Nivelle replaced Pétain in June to turn a defensive posture into a more aggressive one. In July the problem for Falkenhayn and the Germans became clear: they were being bled to death as well, and not only at Verdun. The Allied offensive on the Somme had begun, partly to relieve pressure on Verdun, while the Eastern Front saw Russian resurgence under **Brusilov**. By December, the French forts were recaptured and the Germans were back where they had started. Except that the two sides had suffered over 250,000 killed. A good number of those were around a hill called, fittingly, *Le Mort Homme*.

WF

VERSAILLES

The Treaty of Versailles was signed in the former French royal palace of that name on 28 June 1919, concluding the war with **Germany**. The moment was interpreted in the grand painting by William Orpen, now hanging in IWM London. The treaty had followed months of discussion among the **Allies** at the Paris Peace Conference, led by the 'Big Three' (**Clemenceau** for **France**, **Lloyd George** for Britain and **Wilson** for the **United States**), and separate treaties followed with the other former **Central Powers**. The ramifications of the treaty – particularly as to how far it led to the rise of Hitler and the next global war – are still debated. The politicians of Germany hoped for an 'honourable' settlement respectful of the nation's pre-war status, and one based on **Wilson**'s ideals in his Fourteen Points for a new world order. Instead, Germany – which was not allowed to attend the talks – had to accept a rather different set of terms. The German Army was rolled back to the size of a small home-defence force and was not permitted near the Rhine; it lost its air force (and its navy scuttled itself); it lost Alsace and Lorraine (back to France), as well as territory to **Belgium** and its eastern provinces to an independent Poland; it was forbidden from uniting with Austria; it lost all its colonies; and it had to accept blame for starting the war and therefore pay **reparations** to the Allies. Intolerable though these conditions were for most Germans, and despite initial refusals to sign, there was ultimately no choice. Germany had neither the stomach, nor the strength, to risk the renewal of hostilities.

GR

VICTORIA CROSS

The Victoria Cross (VC) is the highest gallantry award in the British Armed Forces. It was introduced in 1856, and it can be awarded to a serviceman of any rank. During the First World War, over 600 VCs were awarded across the British and Imperial forces – the largest number in any war to date. The first private to receive one was Sidney Godfrey of the Royal Fusiliers, on 23 August 1914. He, along with his battalion, was ordered to hold two bridges to allow other units to retreat. Godfrey kept the enemy at bay for two hours despite being wounded; one bullet was lodged in his skull. The first **Royal Flying Corps** recipient was Lanoe George Hawker in 1915; unfortunately he was killed in 1916 by the **Red Baron**. The youngest recipient during the war was a teenaged sailor, John 'Jack' Cornwell, who was serving as Boy First Class on board HMS *Chester* during the Battle of **Jutland**. He was mortally wounded but continued to carry out his duties and died shortly after the battle, receiving his VC posthumously. One man achieved a unique distinction in the war, winning two VCs: Captain Noel Godfrey Chavasse of the Royal Army Medical Corps. He earned his first on the **Somme** for rescuing men from **no man's land** while he himself was wounded. His second was gained during the **Passchendaele** offensive, where, for nearly two days, he treated and rescued wounded soldiers on the battlefield. But his second was posthumous, for he died of his wounds on 4 August 1917.

DF

VIMY RIDGE *see* CANADA; WESTERN FRONT

WAR MEMORIALS *to* WOMEN

WAR MEMORIALS

As part of the fabric of **remembrance** of the 1914–1918 conflict, war memorials play an important part, whether they are the grand edifices such as Whitehall's Cenotaph or **Belgium**'s Menin Gate, or the much more modest local structures. Memorials can be very diverse in form, ranging from community crosses, obelisks and plaques, to sculpted figures, lych-gates and gardens, or to windows and whole buildings; even paintings can be memorials. In Britain, war memorials up until the nineteenth century tended to be devoted to officers or to regiments. But with the Anglo-Boer War of 1899–1902, large numbers of volunteers joined up, and the community reaction to their deaths led to the first significant memorials to ordinary soldiers. That scale of memorial-building paled into insignificance compared with what was prompted by the First World War. During the war, temporary street shrines with the names of individuals sprang up to acknowledge those fighting abroad. Over time, with the increasing death toll, these were adorned with flowers in memory of those killed. The bodies of the hundreds of thousands who died in the war, from Britain alone, could not be repatriated (even where they could be identified), leaving families and communities with no location for their grief. Thus, war memorials served that function, and people came together to build them in the country's largest ever public art programme. The result of this welter of activity was monuments, rolls of honour and books of remembrance. 'Utilitarian' memorials inscribed with names were popular, too, including hospital beds, organs and clock towers. Factories, banks, government offices, schools and universities, the Post Office and railway companies also created their own memorials. Since then, casualties from later wars have been added to memorials, serving – along with **poppies** – a wider sense of remembrance.

FC

WESTERN FRONT

The Western Front was the decisive battlefield of 1914–1918, and the one most characterised by **trenches**. In some nations' histories it is often taken to stand for the war as a whole, because of the concentration of their men and resources there; and for **France** and **Belgium** the Western Front was, after all, the battle for national salvation. The military cemeteries, memorials and historic battlefields there now stand as testament to the scale of the struggle. Its fighting can be seen as a series of phases. An initial war of movement, as the Germans attempted to enact their **Schlieffen Plan** to knock out France, was followed by the solidification of trench lines, from Flanders to the Swiss border, after the **Allies** pushed back on the **Marne**. Both sides sought ways to advance, and the holy grail was a 'breakthrough' to overcome the stalemate of trench warfare. The years 1915–1916 witnessed large set-piece infantry attacks, the introduction of poison **gas** and the **tank**, and massive, long **artillery** barrages, all of which consumed hundreds of thousands of lives but which modified the front lines by a few miles at most. From those years, the **Somme** and **Verdun** stand out as the names signifying the human sacrifice. In 1917, the Germans snipped out a vulnerable bulge in their own lines by withdrawing to the fortified **Hindenburg Line**. The British experienced mixed fortunes – capturing strategically important sites such as Vimy Ridge and **Messines**, experimenting with new tactics at **Cambrai**, and extending the salient of territory around **Ypres** – before the rains turned the Battle of **Passchendaele** into a nightmare of mud. Meanwhile, an air war raged overhead and units of the French Army, their resilience shattered, were openly mutinying. In 1918 the stalemate truly broke, as the Germans attempted a series of offensives from March 1918, particularly against the British, using their new tactics of brief bombardments and stormtroopers 'infiltrating' enemy lines. Yet the hard-pressed Allies rallied, and the counter-thrust of their **Hundred Days Offensive** – now including the Americans – swept the Germans back all along the front and forced an effective surrender in the shape of the **Armistice** of 11 November.

EC

WILSON

When US President Woodrow Wilson (1856–1924) led his country to war in April 1917, it was the decisive factor in ensuring the **Allies'** ultimate victory. **Germany'**s dwindling resources of manpower and materials could not match this imminent rejuvenation of the Allies' cause. Yet it was with a heavy heart that Wilson took the decision, as he had long been committed to keeping his country neutral, and had tried to mediate between the combatants – even though American arms were being sold to the Allies. However, unrestricted submarine warfare by **U-boats** and the revelations of the **Zimmermann telegram** forced his hand. Nevertheless, Wilson still insisted on higher motives, and his celebrated Fourteen Points for peace were an attempt to create a new democratic world order. They promoted such ideas as national self-determination and a new diplomacy, including a League of Nations, to prevent wars rather than relying on the old balance of powers. By October 1918 Germany was grasping at this as its most advantageous basis for a settlement, but the problem was both the programme's idealistic but vague notions and the rather different ideas of the European Allies – as well as the fact that Wilson struck his fellow leaders as sanctimonious. **Clemenceau** of **France** mused that 'God Himself was content with ten' commandments and that speaking to the aloof Wilson was 'like talking to Jesus Christ'. In the end, the Treaty of **Versailles** had more of victor's justice than Wilson wanted.

Disappointment and illness attended his final years: a stroke in 1919 drastically reduced his influence at home, and although his much-vaunted League of Nations came into being, he could not persuade his own country to join it.

WF

WOMEN

Across the **home fronts** of the nations at war, women found themselves in new roles. In Britain, women's early contributions to the war effort were primarily as **nurses** or in charitable work, with upper- and middle-class ladies leading the way. They raised funds, spent time **knitting** comforts for the troops, wrapped bandages, packed parcels for **POWs** and ran canteens. They also helped with the large influx of Belgian refugees in 1914. Many women sought more active roles, but they often faced resistance from authority. On offering her medical services to the War Office, Dr Elsie Inglis was told: 'Go home and sit still' – until the French government eagerly employed her Scottish Women's Hospitals, where women occupied all roles, from anaesthetists to surgeons. As the war's appetite for **munitions** and supplies became ever greedier, and men volunteered for the front or were conscripted, labour shortages brought all women greater employment opportunities. They took over traditionally male jobs and played a key role in the munitions factories that sprouted around Britain. With the formation of the Women's Land Army in 1917, the number of women working in agriculture rose to 250,000, while transport employed over 117,000 women in stations and on buses and trams – though the drivers tended still to be men. The last two years of war saw the militarisation of women's roles, in the shape of the new Women's Army Auxiliary Corps, Women's Royal Naval Service and Women's Royal Air Force – the 'Waacs', 'Wrens' and 'Penguins'. The sense of a transformation in women's horizons prompted the newly founded **Imperial War Museum** to create a Women's Work Sub-Committee, responsible for collecting information and artefacts that would recognise the significant female contribution to the First World War. And that contribution helped to realise the long campaign for women's right to vote, beginning with the December 1918 General Election, where, for the first time, a proportion of British women were allowed to exercise their choice in the ballot.

SP

X-RAYS

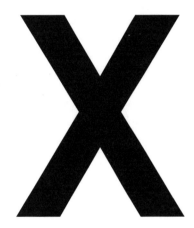

X-RAYS

In 1895 the German scientist Wilhelm Röntgen discovered a kind
of ray that could travel through the human body and produce
photographs of bones. He called these mysterious phenomena
'X-rays', and within a month doctors were using them. Surgeons
could now see where a bullet was lodged rather than having to
probe for it, making it much easier to remove. Both the Germans
and British soon proved the value of X-rays in military surgery,
and by the First World War X-ray machines were in regular
Army use. The Royal Army Medical Corps had six mobile X-ray
units, and the famous Polish-French scientist Marie Curie set up
mobile X-ray units in converted vans, which travelled to the front
where they became known as '*petites Curies*' (little Curies). In her
words, 'The use of the X-rays during the war saved the lives of
many wounded men; it also saved many from long suffering and
lasting infirmity.'

AC

YPRES

YPRES

Ypres, in Flanders, was strategically crucial to the British and the Belgians throughout the war. For the British, Ypres was their Continental backstop, and its loss would likely spell disaster, giving the Germans access to the vital lifelines of Calais, Dunkirk and Boulogne, through which men and supplies passed. And from there England itself could even be threatened. For the Belgians, this corner of Flanders was especially significant as the one part of **Belgium** unoccupied by the Germans: it allowed Belgians to feel they had not been conquered and provided hope for eventual liberation. Three major battles were named after Ypres – the First in 1914, which created this Allied toehold in Flanders; the Second in 1915, where the **Allies** reeled under poison **gas** and the salient shrank; and the Third in 1917, where the Allies took important territory but had to endure the infamously miserable, waterlogged conditions around **Passchendaele**. In April 1918 it was the intense German pressure to break through to the Channel ports and emasculate the **BEF** that prompted Field Marshal Haig's '**Backs to the Wall**' order to his men. But by October 1918, things were very different, and Ypres was comfortably behind the Allied front lines as the war's end neared. Ypres was known to British soldiers as 'Wipers', which lent its name to the most famous of the soldiers' **trench journals**, the *Wipers Times*, written, edited and printed close to the front line. The Menin Gate, commemorating over 54,000 British and Imperial soldiers who have no known grave, was unveiled in the town in 1927; and that year the 'Last Post' was played for the first time, by the Buglers of the Ypres Fire Brigade, in a daily ritual that still continues today.

HB

ZEPPELIN *to* ZIMMERMANN TELEGRAM

ZEPPELIN

Most weapons in the war were intended for the battlefield, but the Zeppelin achieved its notoriety in British eyes for its bombing campaign over England's cities and towns. In 1915, with the **Royal Navy**'s blockade beginning to bite, **Germany** decided to hit Britain's **home front** from the air, and that meant using the range and carrying capacity of airships. The Zeppelin, named after its inventor, was a lighter-than-air craft, whose rigid metal frame was covered with over 2,000 sheets made of cow's intestines to form cells. These were filled with hydrogen to provide lift. In January 1915, airships commenced their campaign, bombing coastal towns in Norfolk, and in May Zeppelins struck London. Attacking at night, the Zeppelins could not navigate or bomb very accurately, so targeting was primitive and civilians died. The public were frightened and outraged, and the government was alarmed. One wartime diarist noted: 'There are no civilians now, we are all soldiers'. Airships were frustratingly difficult to counter until night-fighters of the **Royal Flying Corps** were armed with machine guns firing new incendiary bullets. But it was not until the night of 2–3 September 1916 that William Leefe Robinson scored the defenders' first success, destroying airship *SL.11* and its crew near London, and earning a VC for his bravery. Despite further successes by the British defenders, German Navy airships persevered with – increasingly ineffective – raids until August 1918, while the German Army turned to bombing Britain more efficiently with its newly-developed Gotha **aeroplanes**. In total, the 57 airship raids on Britain killed 564 people and injured another 1,370 – as compared to the 835 deaths and over 1,990 injuries caused by 27 Gotha raids.

SW

ZIMMERMANN TELEGRAM

The Zimmermann telegram (16 January 1917) was a coded diplomatic note by German Under-Secretary of State Arthur Zimmermann to the German Minister (ambassador) in Mexico. But this bald description belies its real importance, for it was a catalyst of war. British intelligence intercepted the message, deciphered it and recognised its explosive nature: the question was – how to use the information? In the telegram, the German Minister was asked to investigate the chances of a German–Mexican military agreement in case the **United States** entered the war; it proposed German funding for Mexico and support for a Mexican effort to regain territories that had been incorporated into the United States. British intelligence did not want to reveal they were listening in to German cable traffic, so they managed to plausibly claim the telegram was obtained from a spy in Mexico. It was passed to the United States in February 1917. Together with Germany's renewal of unrestricted submarine warfare, the telegram had a fundamental effect on US public opinion and helped to mobilise US support for war. That decision was taken by President **Wilson** and the US Congress in April 1917. The affair was a major coup for British intelligence.

MS

LIST OF CONTRIBUTORS

Alan Wakefield
Amy Foulds
Andrew Calver
Anna Lotinga
Anthony Richards
Bryony Phillips
Carl Warner
Charlotte Czyzyk
Christopher Sharpe
Craig Murray
Daniel Francis
Edgar Aromin
Eleanor Ferguson
Eleanor Hilton
Ellen Parton
Emily Charles
Frances Casey
George Jordan
Grant Rogers
Helen Blakeborough
Helen Mavin
Hilary Roberts
Ian Proctor
Jamie Vincent
Karen Gurney
Kate Crowther
Laura Wilkinson
Lee D. Murrell

Lynsey Martenstyn
Maria Payne
Mark Whitmore
Martin Anthony
Matthew John Pentlow
Michael Schmalholz
Natasha Wallace
Nicolas Vanderpeet
Philip Sawford
Philip W. Deans
Rachael Hodson
Rachana Gautam
Rachel Donnelly
Rebecca Louise Harding
Robert William Rumble
Robin Revell
Samantha Clarkson
Samantha Jolley
Sarah Paterson
Shirelle Hawkins
Simon Robbins
Stephen Woolford
Suzanne Bardgett
Terry Charman
Tom O'Keeffe
Victoria Thompson
William Fowlis

FURTHER READING

1914–1918: The History of the First World War
David Stevenson (Penguin, 2012)

The First World War: A Very Short Introduction
Michael Howard (OUP Oxford, 2007)

The First World War
Hew Strachan (Simon & Schuster, 2003)

Forgotten Victory: The First World War, Myth and Realities
Gary Sheffield (Headline Book Publishing, 2001)

The Great War
Ian FW Beckett (Routledge, 2007)

The Great War: Myth and Memory
Dan Todman (London: Hambledon Continuum, 2007)

The Imperial War Museum Book of the First World War
Malcolm Brown (London: Sidgwick & Jackson, 1991)

The Imperial War Museum Book of the Western Front
Malcolm Brown (London: Sidgwick & Jackson, 1993).
Republished in paperback by Pan in 2001.

The Myriad Faces of War: Britain and the Great War, 1914–1918
Trevor Wilson (Cambridge: Polity Press, 1986).
Republished by Faber & Faber in 2010.

Tommy: the British Soldier on the Western Front, 1914–1918
Richard Holmes (London: HarperCollins, 2004)

ACKNOWLEDGEMENTS

With thanks to all contributors for their enthusiasm. Special
thanks are due to Terry Charman and Mark Hawkins-Dady.
Thanks also to Madeleine James, Caitlin Flynn, Elizabeth
Bowers, Sarah Paterson and all other IWM staff who have
helped to make this book possible.

Extracts from *Great Contemporaries* by Sir Winston Churchill
reproduced with permission of Curtis Brown, London on
behalf of the Estate of Sir Winston Churchill, copyright
© Winston S. Churchill. With thanks to David Higham
Associates for permission to quote from *The First World War –
An Illustrated History* by A J P Taylor (Penguin).